Therapeutic Madness, a nonfiction

narrative, chronicles my dramatic journey through eleven months of psychotherapy undertaken in pursuit of healing myself—after three previous attempts—from the life shattering effects of an anxiety disorder which caused me to resign my faculty position at a well known university. This is the story of how I made my "great recovery" from a hermit–like existence back into the wider world...and how others can do it, too.

The complex relationship between my therapist, wife, and myself makes for engrossing and compelling reading. Yet, it is not the driving theme I present. Rather, the heart of my story is the healing which is played out against this **madness**. Those readers interested in self–help and God's working in the healing process will be intrigued by my obsessive compulsive disorder, an anxiety disorder whose "remission" was the result of my self–analysis program motivated and sustained by deep faith as contrasted against the therapeutic process.

What happened to me illustrates the important need for accountability in psychiatry and therapy in general. Chapter twenty reviews the writings of therapy experts who hold a similar viewpoint.

For forty years I led a normal life, much like most people. Then it happened, an insidious depression led me into an anxiety disorder. I sought help from those whom I thought knew how to help...but....

Dedicated to the *Throw Away Dead*

Recently, a brief article in the Atlanta Constitution referenced the "refurbishing" of the graveyard at a huge state run mental institution in the United States. The article explained that the refurbishing was actually the establishment of a memorial for those who had gone to this place for care and had died there. This memorial, a result of the action of friends and former patients, was to mark the fact that some thirty thousand people, yes that is correct, 30,000 fellow humans, were buried there. Many of them were buried in graves so shallow that only inches of soil covered their "resting" place. Each person had been buried "Without a Name"— in a grave marked only by a number!

Therapeutic

Madness

John I. Lynch

◘ *Verlager Books*

Published 1998

Cover by Matt Wuerker
Library of Congress Cataloging-in-Publication Data
Lynch, John I., 1948
          Therapeutic Madness / John I. Lynch
                    p.   cm.
          Includes bibliography references
          ISBN 0-9660249-0-7
1. Healing mental disorders. 2. Psychotherapy patient abuse.
3. Antipsychiatry. 4. Psychotherapy–moral and ethical aspects.
5. Consumer education. 6. Faith and Healing.
          RC438.5M345
          DMLM/DLC
          for Library of Congress   97-091126

Introduction

My story possesses a particular characteristic. It comes into focus without announcement or awareness as it unfolds: not suddenly, but quietly, almost imperceptibly. Like random pieces of a puzzle—each a different shape and size—the events, people, and ideas come together in a meaningful form. First a corner, then a side, and finally the entire border falls into place. But the scene is not immediately clear.

Pages will flow by and as they do more sections fit together. Meaningfulness starts to emerge. By the end the picture is obvious. My words put a frame around my particular scene which is Obsessive Compulsive Disorder, psychological healing through faith and self–analysis writing, and therapeutic madness. Within these pages appear truths for all people facing today's demands.

Here the rigorous and complex journey into my subconscious mind starts. The following image crystallizes my psychological state: I stand looking down a flight of steps representing levels of my subconscious. The further I descend the more anxious I become. I am profoundly unsettled and to escape this feeling I obsess about it until the anxiety is reduced. By then, however, the next step down is reached and the process continues. My story compares to such an image: I travel down a metaphorical flight of stairs which leads me deeper and deeper into my subconscious and eventually into a kind of therapeutic madness. At my lowest point, I am challenged either to heal myself, that is to extricate myself from the quagmire of psychotherapy, by becoming in essence my own therapist, or not do so and perhaps pay a terrible price.

CHAPTER 1

Daily Life with Obsessive Compulsive Disorder
The year was 1988 and I was driving home on the autobahn between Wiesbaden and Stuttgart in Germany. As I drove my thoughts turned to the statistics course I had just taught. Without a doubt, I had made a dismal showing of my teaching skills by teaching the entire course without writing on the blackboard. I had failed my students and myself. Why? Fear of catching AIDS from a blackboard. My irrational thinking told me someone with AIDS had contaminated it.

What concerned me even more was that this was not the first time I had been unfair to my students. In a previous course, a student with a cut finger had placed his paper in my briefcase; I became frightened of AIDS contamination and threw the entire briefcase away destroying many hours of student homework. This course, just finished, was my last desperate attempt to fight my illness. My desire to move forward with my life was not to be—I realized this in a moment of lucid insight. And then, in just an instant, I decided to end the pain of my recurring failure and resigned my university position.

The academics of Obsessive Compulsive Disorder (OCD) never interested me, perhaps like a cancer patient who doesn't care about the academics of cancer. Living with OCD is enough. In some ways I am probably like many OCD people, and in other ways, I suspect, there are differences. Surely, we have this in common: not telling others about the disorder and disguising OCD behaviors. Like most OCD persons there are "obsessions," or unwanted thoughts and worries, and there are "compulsions," which are behaviors done to relieve the obsessional tension. In my case the obsession is fear of catching AIDS, and the compulsion is mostly hand washing. The result is: withdrawal from life!

Almost everything in my tormented world has to be

scrutinized to make sure it is not contaminated by AIDS carrying blood—doorknobs, shopping bags, groceries, and clothing, to name a few. Though I have read about AIDS extensively and have listened to the experts, this fear cannot be shaken for it is highly irrational and does not yield to logic and information. And I deeply worry that I will end up like Howard Hughes who obsessively controlled his environment by never leaving his bed. All his riches, his keen intelligence, and his grand accomplishments couldn't prevent Obsessive Compulsive Disorder from destroying his life.

Consider the following illustration: There are ten million needles in a box but only one is contaminated with AIDS infected blood. A billion dollar reward will be given to anyone willing to be stuck with a randomly drawn needle. Hopefully, my idea presents you with the criteria of "risk and reward," which define so much of life. Taking the risk seems logical if you need the money. In my case, however, even if there are a trillion needles in the box and even if I am utterly destitute, I won't allow myself to be pricked. Why? My AIDS risk/reward criteria fall far outside normal parameters. In other aspects of my life, the balance between risk and reward is within normal limits. For example, I will drive at one hundred miles an hour on German autobahns, climb to high places, and swim in extemely deep water. To sum it up: my OCD—induced AIDS fear is illogical and can't be rationally thought away, for I have tried. To provide insight into my housebound life with OCD let me describe daily life.

I live in a house with my wife Beth and our dog Laurie, where only an occasional friend and almost never a stranger is allowed to enter. The house is as clean and neat as Beth makes it; my OCD contamination fear prevents me from doing housekeeping. For example, if a piece of paper falls on the floor it lies there. It is a difficult time for Beth who has a demanding job and a demanding OCD spouse. As I continue to describe my daily life, two words come to mind: worry and fear. All my days are spent within the confines of worry and fear.

My day begins when I awake in the only place where there is freedom from AIDS fear: my bed. Although sleeping my life away would be pleasurable, I arise at 9 A.M. after sleeping ten hours. Every behavior from this point must be orderly; for example, I dress sequentially: socks first, shirt next, then pants, and finally shoes. Anything out of sequence, like putting my shoes on first, will break the ritual, escalate the AIDS contamination fear, and increase obsessional anxiety. Therefore, my shoes and clothing are placed within reach of the bed in an orderly fashion. Standing on the bare floor without wearing shoes to protect my feet is impossible, so I dress myself standing on a clean white towel. Putting my pants on poses a special problem. If by accident a cuff touches the carpet, my sequence is broken and I must get a pair of clean pants. Then the ritual of dressing begins again.

I am never in a hurry to get dressed because the difficulty of making breakfast lies ahead. Ritualistic hand washing begins here. After entering the kitchen, the cleanest counter top is selected. Any visible speck of dirt on a counter top forces me to wash my hands, wash that speck off, and then rewash my hands after washing off the faucet. Only then can my breakfast, which consists of tea and toast, be prepared. Everything, like dressing, must be done in a certain order. First, a loaf of bread is taken from the refrigerator and placed on the counter; then my hands are washed again. Next, a plate is selected from the kitchen cabinet. If this plate has a water spot or speck of food on it, another plate must be taken—a contamination free plate must be found. After selecting the plate my hands are washed, the bread is placed on it, my hands are washed again, and so on. There were days when five plates had been selected before a suitable one was discovered.

Think of me sitting eating toast. I touch the plate and, alas, remember that my hands haven't been washed after the plate was placed on the table. The toast and plate must now be put in the sink, and I must start again to look for a clean plate. Here the obsession is believing my food is contaminated with the AIDS (HIV) virus while the compulsion is to keep washing my hands to assuage the obsession: a vicious cycle if there ever is one. And one that requires constant thinking: my mind never rests.

Rational thinking says, "Just eat your toast you're not going to catch AIDS from it." There were days when I did fight through fear and defy rituals. But OCD made me pay a powerful price for confronting it: my fear of catching AIDS dramatically increased and obsessional anxiety rose causing me to feel like a patient sitting in a doctor's office waiting for cancer test results. This anxiety could last for minutes, hours, or even days. Living with rituals became easier than living with defiance anxiety. This day before finishing breakfast, my hands have been washed ten times.

Most days are spent home alone with our dog, Laurie. Fortunately, there is a small fenced yard so she can go out herself. Laurie lays on the couch and sleeps or just looks at me watching television. Television is my sedative but it contributes nothing to my mental health. If the phone rings, I let it ring. When I hear a knock at the door, I ignore it unless I know someone is stopping by. Of course, there are practical exceptions, for example, if Beth has said she will be calling. Still, my ear never touches the receiver; AIDS fears are everywhere.

The highlight of my day occurs when Beth returns from work. She is the support I need to venture out, if only for an hour. I feel terrible about being unable to pet and play with Laurie, but once Beth returns we can all take our daily walk.

Protecting myself from AIDS is more complicated outside the house. My perceptual skills are acute—a cut finger, a gum wrapper, a piece of tissue, or a cigarette butt can be sighted from a great distance. All these things are associated with AIDS and contamination. As we walk Beth reassures me and helps me look for pieces of tissue, band-aids, and the like.

By now the nature of the OCD mind set should be apparent, but let me fine-tune this understanding a bit. Let us suppose that I step within three inches of a tissue before seeing it. After this, I will obsess and constantly ask Beth if I have stepped on it. Her reassurance is desperately needed. She always gives it to me. Still, I question her again and ask her for more reassurance. I may even walk back to the tissue and retrace my steps at least once, perhaps twice, maybe even ten times. You see, constant reassurance and ritualistic behavior are the only ways obsessional anxiety can be reduced; otherwise, an agonizing relentless anxiety will drive me to bed.

Occasionally things are perfect and my walk gives me an opportunity to declare a small victory. Most often, however, OCD defeats me. Usually something has happened, I have stepped too near a band-aid, piece of paper, or beer bottle—a stranger has petted our dog or Laurie has met another dog, so by the time we return home, I am obsessing, and Beth is anxious and distraught. Then to make matters worse, Beth has to disinfect my shoes and give Laurie a bath.

The evening meal is less difficult for me because Beth prepares it. Now there are only obsessions about eating the meal, not making it, and hand washing is not as necessary. Thank God that Beth is such a good facilitator and does things for me. Without her help I could never have found enough strength to continue my struggle against OCD.

Bathing and personal hygiene require the highest level of orderliness. Our house has three bathrooms, mine is private. Even Beth isn't allowed to use my bathroom. When bathing and showering everything must be arranged in the right order: a special unused soap and a lint free white towel are required. If I notice the tiniest piece of lint after taking a shower, I must shower again and dry off with another towel. There are many evenings when four consecutive showers will be taken before I can climb into bed.

Within the OCD morass, a sense of normalcy is found in

my sexual relations. Having conjugal relations with Beth represents a triumph of my will over OCD and shows me that there is a limit to OCD controlled behavior. Of course, our sexual relationship represents love and caring but in a special way it also represents the hope that other things can change. If this limit can be set, then why not others?

OCD isn't keeping one's house and dresser drawers in order. It is a complex and debilitating disorder that can thoroughly isolate a functioning child or adult. Beth has been encouraging me for months to give therapy another chance. At first I resisted, after all, my previous therapies haven't helped much. Yet now, I am tired of being sick and feel emotionally stronger, so I agree to try again. And I, certainly, believe in my mind's capacity to heal itself if the right "guide" is found and followed.

CHAPTER 2

My OCD escape begins on a fine warm spring day at University Medical Center Psychiatric Associates in Forrest, New Island. The large group practice has a staff of twenty psychiatrists, fourteen residents, and several practitioners. I am scheduled through the crisis and brief therapy clinic.

For several days I obsess about possibly catching AIDS in the hospital, and I tell myself to cancel this appointment. Nevertheless, the day arrives and the hour long drive to the hospital is made.

As Beth leads me toward the hospital entrance, I become more and more anxious—there are too many gum spots and pieces of debris on the walkway for my liking. A revolving door and a hinged door now confront me: which to choose? The revolving door is avoided because I don't want to touch anything. Beth opens the other door and we enter the hospital. Here I am. My steps are carefully placed because the carpeted floor can't be washed with an antiseptic and seems spotted with blood.

The short walk to the third floor psychiatry department is painful; my stomach is wrenching and churning because the odds for healing are against me. But an insightful therapist, I reassure myself, may be able to change them. This therapist will be my fourth. After three unsuccessful therapies, I know what is needed, an active plan for getting better, and what isn't, a directionless therapist who just sits and listens: interaction not passivity shall be my direction and no long term medications for me. Maybe this time....

Session 4/28

Soon I am standing nervously in the waiting room's corner feeling ambivalent and frightened. My appointment is for three o'clock. At ten past Beth hears me mutter, my body drained of courage, "I'm leaving!"At this very moment a dark haired woman arrives and introduces herself as Grace Tyre.

She reaches to shake hands; my quivering hand stays safely by my side. Her hand falls back, and she guides us to her office.

After carefully scanning it for OCD dangers, my seat is selected with trepidation. I ruminate about who has previously sat on this chair. Her office is hostile territory: it is dimly lit, the walls are colorless, the office furniture is old, and there are sordid looking carpet spots—has dried blood caused them?

"Why are you here?" Grace asks adjusting her ankle length dress. Then she picks up a pen and yellow note pad from her desk.

"Because I have Obsessive Compulsive Disorder," I answer, with eyes scanning for missed AIDS dangers.

"Can you describe your OCD for me?" queries Grace.

Anxiety floods me with nervous energy as I reveal, in sort of a detached trance, how OCD decimated my professional career, encapsulated my social life, and forced Beth to retire from the Air Force Nurse Corps. I continue, my nerves edgy, and tell her about my failed therapies.... It's always difficult to recall my mournful and never–ending OCD saga: today is no different.

As the session unfolds, Grace asks, "Why are you returning to psychiatry at this time?"

"To get better, of course," condescendingly I comeback in an arrogant tone. Maybe she'll reject me with a counter arrogance, then, I can justify not returning; that's OCD logic.

She shrugs her shoulders in a suit yourself gesture and says, "That's what we're here for."

Beth sits and listens to the dialogue patiently waiting to speak, but Grace doesn't ask her any questions. After twenty minutes Grace glances at her desk clock and says, "I want to tell you I'm a resident who works half–time and I'm only here one and a half days a week. The other day I work at a local clinic." She places her pad on the desk and comments, "My supervisor will review your case and then assign a permanent psychiatrist. Dr. Tom, the residency director, may take you on. He's a brilliant man and OCD specialist." Then there is a long pause. After which, she inquires, her eyes sharp with interest, "Will you accept a resident? Perhaps, I'll decide to ask for you."

"Sure," I answer quickly using wry humor to break internal tension, "a resident will be all right since this isn't brain surgery." She ends the interview after twenty–five minutes with directions to call her secretary and make an appointment. As we navigate the hospital minefield, I am feeling worse every minute, so I make nothing but redundant, fearful, AIDS remarks to Beth as we walk to our car.

*Dr. Tyre's notes unedited—My comments are noted in **bold**.

4/28 Initial Assessment Chief Complaint
   Chief Complaint: "I can't open doors. . . I'm immobilized by OCD" History of Present Illness: This is a 50 year old, married, ergonomics professor disabled by OCD with onset 1984 in San Francisco centering around fears of contracting Aids. He notes no urgent change in status: "I'm always an emergency patient" **(Never)** for years but lives in near total isolation with only his wife on a farm which he seldom leaves. He recently needed a dental procedure but refused a routine cleaning to accompany it—he prioritizes that preserving a tooth is worth the extreme anxiety of dental visits but routine care is not—and wound up in conflict with the dentist. This experience made him decide to again risk leaving his home enclave to seek psychiatric help. **(Not true)**
   Past Psychiatric history and Treatment. Psychiatric therapy times 3—each time he felt symptoms worsened. Attempted behavioral medicine times 1, found it unbearable at first session. Anafranil times months–marked improvement in symptoms, constipation and other side effects intolerable. Developmental// Personal History: Wife RN in service **(Not true, retired for 6 years)**
   Mental Status Exam a) General appearance and behavior: three–day grizzled beard **(Worn beard for 15 years)**, uncombed longish hair, withdrew when I approached **(I don't shake hands, ever)**, but then cooperative. Dress and hygiene appeared otherwise

appropriate. Eye contact good. b) Speech: normal rate rhythm prosody. c) Mood: anxious. d) Affect: full, congruent; initially argumentative, cantankerous, then becoming increasingly relaxed, frequent and spontaneous humor. e) Thought content/process: (including homicidal ideation, suicidal ideation and psychotic). Logical and coherent negative SI, negative HI, negative audio and visual hallucinations, negative delusions. f) Cognitive functioning: grossly above average, good insight, judgment, abstraction. Assessment and formulation: fifty-year old with long history of OCD to which he has adjusted well by totally limiting his exposure to the world . . . has had limited med **(Medication)** trials. Is not clear if he is willing to try meds again, but is interested in supportive (not insight-oriented psychiatric) therapy; need more evaluation to gather history, explore goals.

DSM III **(Diagnostic & Statistical Manual)**—R Axis I—OCD Axis II—deferred Axis III——none. Treatment Goals and Plan; 1. Evaluate or evaluation to explore diagnosis and treatment. 2. No urgent meds/treatment needed. 3. Patient has CBTs **(Crisis and Brief Therapy Clinic)** number if necessary.

Beth and I discuss Grace on our return home and agree about her positive signs. She wears a wedding band so there will be less fear of catching AIDS from her. Another positive sign, she is young and may have a flexible therapeutic approach. Finally, I like her dark attractive eyes and her shapeless ankle length black print dress which gave her an interesting 60's look. A verse from the Book of Hebrews comes to mind: "Now faith is the substance of things hoped for, the evidence of things not seen." Yes, I hope she will accept me as her patient.

Today, I leave for therapy with a mangled mind leaking away in lonely, wasteful OCD self–conflict.

Session 5/26

Beth waits with me hugging her side in the reception room corner. I am having a mental assessment which requires a two hour appointment. Nervous, worrying, alone without Beth, Grace and I walk to her office. Once seated Grace asserts, "I've decided to accept you as my patient." Then she asks, "What do you expect in therapy?"

"I've no interest in psychotherapy," I reply firmly, as she begins writing on a notepad. "What I'm looking for is an interactive therapist. Someone who will provide me with encouragement." I hesitate watching for her reaction, but it is nothing graphic. Then I continue, "And someone who will help me explore the more positive aspects of my life. You know, see me as more than an OCD or neurotic mind and a psychiatric diagnosis, like my last psychiatrist and childhood family doctor did."

"You should know," responds Grace, raising her voice from its soft pitch, casting a slight smile, "that my goal is to get you back into life as quickly as possible. Also, the very nature of therapy is changing; for instance, we're planning on starting a program here at University where a patient will be assigned more than one psychiatrist...."

"That sounds encouraging," I remark.

Next she asks, "What is your ideal therapy schedule?"

"I'd like two appointments a week combined into one–two hour session. Walking through the hospital twice a week is too stressful for me. And meeting for two hours will give me time to unwind from the stress of coming." Memories have forced their way into my mind; anxiously I pause and look at the dried flowers hanging on the wall. Then I unsurely go on, "My last two therapists thought the stress of coming to the hospital made me focus on my AIDS contamination fear. By having longer sessions, they believed I would participate more effectively in the process.... And I found their words were right on. You know," I continue rather boldly, "they recognized the complexity of an OCD mind and the difficulty in reaching it." Grace doesn't respond, so I sit there for a moment watching her, wondering why she doesn't agree.

Then she says, "I'll have to think about our schedule!" and makes a note of it on her pad.

"It sure would be helpful if you could arrange my schedule this way. I'd...."

"Tell me," Grace interrupts at my hesitation, "something

about your family life."

"My father is overbearing and verbally aggressive and my mother is manipulative. But I have a wonderful grandmother and some other relatives I'm close to."

As we talk about my family and psychiatric history, I seek a condition of emotional numbness. Unfortunately, it's too long a distance from OCD anxiety to numbness, so I go only from incredulity to chagrin. We talk along the outer rim of psychological escarpment for awhile, but I won't look anymore into the chasm. Grace places her pad and pen on her desk telling me the session is over. "We'll meet next Thursday at eleven if that's good for you," she remarks and reaches for an appointment card.

"I'll remember it," I quickly reply to her; no way am I touching anything she touches. Grace opens her office door; then she leads me down the hallway and opens that door. I step into the corridor where Beth's calming presence awaits me.

A dangerous trek home lies ahead; perhaps, I will step on a band–aid or a tissue while walking through the hospital or parking lot. If so, I will be an emotional wreck for a week and never return.

Session 5/26 Two hour psychiatric therapy

Chief complaint: "OCD... AIDS is my big stumbling block." History of Present Illness (see my note of 4/28) This is a 50 year old married disabled ergonomics professor who has had OCD since the early 80's, marked by obsessions of AIDS contamination, compulsions of hand washing in the past and now by compulsive avoidance to the extent that the pt lives with his wife in near isolation on a farm in Maine and in Florida, depending on the season. He does not work, shop, socialize, receive routine health care, etc., but describes his ability to move around his farm as being nearly normal, i.e. he is able to touch objects without excessive hand washing on most days.

Goals for treatment—Patient would like to work for recovery from OCD although this is very anxiety provoking to contemplate for him. Is willing to try meds and eventually, cognitive behavioral therapy. Motivation: fear of what will happen if wife becomes sick/unable to care for him. No symptoms MDE. (**Major depressive episode**)

Past psychiatric history: Has had three different treatments 1. Insight oriented therapy in the mid 80's. Felt his symptoms got much worse during the course of this. 2. Behavioral medicine: Increased anxiety associated with initial goal setting, did not follow through. Not on any meds at the time. 3. Anafranil times months with improvement in symptoms but severe constipation time. 4. Family medical and psychiatric history: OCD—patient believes mother and father both have undiagnosed OCD, live very circumscribed lives.

Development/personal history: Grew up in Pittsburgh Father "emotionally abusive" of patient and mother name calling. Has one younger brother. (Second Mental Status exam, first regular appointment) a) General appearance/behavior. No change from previous exam; grizzled three–day beard, uncombed hair, appropriate dress and hygiene otherwise. Good eye contact, no psychiatric motor changes. Cooperative, assertive without hostility b) Speech: normal rate, volume, prosody. c) Mood: very anxious. d) Affect: Full congruent, mildly anxious, frequent appropriate dry humor. e) Thought Content/Process: Logical and coherent negative for suicidal ideation, negative homicidal ideation, negative for audio and visual hallucination, negative delusions. f) Cognitive function: Grossly above average intelligence, excellent abstraction, excellent insight and judgment.

Assessment and formulation: 50 year old with long established OCD and fairly comfortable adjustment to the diagnosis by living enclaved life; who now wishes to address his symptoms albeit with some emotional ambivalence. DSM III–R Axis I OCD Axis II deferred Treatment Goals and Plans: 1. Continue to build rapport. 2. Begin psychoeducation regarding OCD and consider teaching regarding Aids. 3. Initiate medical treatment once compliance seems likely–SSRI. (**Selective serotonin reuptake medication**) 4. Cognitive Behavioral Therapy once compliance seems likely.

Session 6/6

Entering the psychiatric reception area I immediately notice an emaciated, fragile looking man sitting in a wheelchair. He is a patient, no doubt, dying of AIDS. The sight of him causes my anxiety level to reach a new height. He looks distraught and I feel distraught. "Why would a dying person," I ask myself, "want to talk with a psychiatrist? What comfort does psychiatry really offer him? He should talk with God to find salvation, or is psychiatry a bit of god in itself to some?"

I reflect on how short life is and how little time there is for me to get well. These thoughts echo in my mind as Grace arrives promptly, as requested. Her smile makes me feel calmer. Had she not arrived on time, my anxiety might have overburdened me; there are just too many fear stimuli in the reception area, too many people coming and going. We enter her office and the protection it now offers.

Grace remarks after we sit, "OCD is a genetic–based disease; therefore, you should take prescription medication instead of doing psychotherapy. Psychotherapy," she continues, "is not considered the best treatment for OCD...."

"Medication," I reply abruptly, having already decided it's not for me, "has serious side effects and doesn't provide a cure. Don't you believe in the mind's potential to heal itself?" Grace leans back in her chair, crosses her legs, adjusts her long brown dress, and stares. Her wordless affect seems confrontational. "Why," I ponder feeling puzzled, "doesn't she expound her position?" Perhaps, that's a sign I should change the subject. So I tell her of my difficult relationship with my parents; then I describe an interaction with a dentist who refused to examine my teeth without a cleaning.

"He knew teeth cleaning provoked my OCD anxiety, but he didn't care," I begin slowly, my nerves twitching. "He had already treated me several times and didn't require a cleaning. I was the most perfect patient—too scared to be anything else—even started brushing my teeth four times a day," a wry bit of humor to relax my jittery nerves is presented, but Grace maintains her stern, staring look. "I complained to the state human rights office who sent out a lawyer to investigate. She wrote up a factual report which stated he must accommodate me, but the board that is made up of politically appointed

lawyers overruled their investigator and gave me no reason."
By now I'm empathizing with other people who are treated
like this, so I snap, "You know how politics work in this
provincial state!" Then I speak less anxiously, "Beth found
me another dentist that is very accommodating, and he
doesn't require a preexamination teeth cleaning. So it all
turned out for the best." Grace remains statue like, wordless.

Speaking like this creates the image of me helplessly
scripting my own destruction in a Hamlet like scene where he
tells how his life has crumbled, how everything is diseased,
how all his interests are morbid. The exact scene I acted for
previous psychiatrists as they encouraged me to talk about my
crumbling life. Perhaps, thinking sardonically, all these
therapists wanted was for me to bring in a skull and recite a
death soliloquy.

Here I enter Grace's silence and ask myself, "Am I
struggling against the basic nature of psychotherapy? Is it
antithetical to my therapeutic needs? This is only the third
session, and already the psychotherapeutic process discour-
ages me. Am I involving myself in a no–win situation?
Maybe, I can't face reality? Then, again, a desperate man does
desperate things!"

I speak uneasy in the silence and tell her more about my
life....

"The session's over. See you next Thursday at...," she
says, interrupting me. Then Grace opens the hallway door,
and I trudge fearfully down the corridor wondering, "Is
therapy worth it, or more than that, or worth nothing at all."

Session 6/6 One hour psychiatric therapy

Continues stable, but with complaint of increasing anxiety with
sessions. Goals: 1. To increase activities of daily living to include
shopping, banking, and other routines; 2. Resume playing tennis.
Does not expect complete remission. Also suggests that education
regarding Aids may be useful. Expresses reluctance regarding
medications– "I'm not a believer in drugs"–but willing to educate
self and consider medications seriously.

Additional History: OCD symptoms date to childhood, but

with hiatus in college; heavy alcohol **(Weekends, mostly at fraternity parties)** at that time, minimal since currently one beer/day max. College–Ph.D. 1977 Ergonomics. Tennis Pro 1972 through 1975. Ergonomic professor 1980–1984 **(1981–1989)**.

O **(Objectively seen)**: Unshaven **(Still have beard)**, anxious (mild–moderate), logical and coherent A/P **(Assessment/Plan)**: Stable OCD setting realistic goals, engaging. Will provide patient with detailed written information regarding prescription for OCD next week. RTC **(Return to clinic)** one week.

On the way home Beth uplifts my spirits by firmly saying, "Grace can delineate the process as she wishes. Remember how Manuel did it! He was a very facilitating and interactive therapist!"

"You may be right," I reply as we turn into our driveway. "Grace has told me how eclectic her treatment methods are and how the very nature of therapy has been changed." Grace has, nevertheless, been quite indecisive, so to get the process moving, I send her a letter redefining my need for an interactive, facilitating therapist.

Today feeling vaguely optimistic and realizing that I might be at a mid–point between the past and future, I leave for therapy.

Session 6/13

As the session begins, Grace says with detachment, "I've decided we will meet for one hour weekly not two." She pauses, her unadorned eyes looking for my reaction which is detachment. Then she proceeds, "I must deny your time request because I am too empathetic as a person. The longer we meet the more empathetic I will become." She leans back in her chair. "Also," she continues, "OCD patients are emotionally manipulative, and you will be less manipulative in a one hour session."

"Aren't all people," I defend, softly, not liking this label and worrying about the implication, "manipulative and controlling by nature?" Now I think, "Tender persuasion may help."

"That's true," she grants with a slight shrug of her

shoulders, "but people with OCD are more so." I nervously wait for a better explanation but none is forthcoming as she remarks, "I think it's best we only meet for one hour and that's how it will be...."

"Have you received my letter?" I now ask.

"No, I don't go to my mailbox everyday. Tell me what's in it," she replies with a broad smile appearing.

I review my role defining letter that asks for a friendly therapist. To my delight, Grace says, "It's good that you are taking an interest in your therapy. Why don't you continue to make suggestions about therapy's direction." She pauses, thinks for a second, slowly shakes her head, and replies, "But I can't make a decision about my role until I think about it." Why does she keep concealing her mind and confusing mine? I wonder. The wisdom of my appeal hasn't touched her to the quick, for sure.

We discuss my OCD for sometime. My deepest thoughts are hidden behind a sheath of impermeability, so I ramble in the superficial. Today, there's no ache from my expressions.

"Will you try some medication?" she asks as the session ends.

"Give me a prescription for a few pills, and if I feel the need, I'll take them." She writes me a prescription for Prozac. Her affect mirrors delight as she hands me the prescription paper. I don't like touching it. The session ends as I think, "I'm not content to leave things as they are."

Session 6/13 One hour psychiatric therapy
Patient obtained for himself and read guide on OCD from the OCD information center; presented me with his underlined and annotated copy. Discussed his reluctance to take medications. Patient feels he will rebel if railroaded into it. Also concerned regarding need to make actual improvement, not just decrease symptoms through medications. Willing to try Paxil however. **(Medication error: prescription was for Prozac)** O: Unshaven **(Still have beard)** Affect full, incongruent humor. Able to take script **(Prescription)** directly from me. A/P: Stable Engaging in therapy Patient will send script to his insurance mail–in service, we

will fully discuss risks–benefits at next meeting–patient will not start before then. RTC 2 week.

For several days my mood toward therapy is hopeful—at least there is an opportunity for me to guide it. Grace, I believe, understands my strong need for a facilitating and interactive therapist, but I realize there must also be a plan for my OCD progress.

Is my road to be drug therapy? Psychotherapy? I seem to resist both. No doubt about it in my mind, if another road can be found, I will take it! To paraphrase Robert Frost: Will that make all the difference?

Session 6/20

Grace greets me in the reception area with, "How are you doing today?" and a broad smile.

"Fine," I answer.

Then she animatedly asks, obviously remembering that I like gardening, "Did you have a nice week gardening?"

"Yes, I did."

"Are you an organic gardener?" she inquires as we walk to her office.

"How did you know?" I reply, my curiosity piqued through apprehension.

"I just know it," she replies, tilting her head slightly and reflecting an air of confidence.

"I've a special interest in ornamental plants," she says. Her expression, pleasurable. "Working with them is fun...," hesitating, "fascinating...."

"Do you grow vegetables, too?" I ask unfolding my hands and lounging back in my chair.

"Not many, mostly ornamentals."

Grace asks me about my college days and I ask about hers. "I was an anthropology major at Yale...," she answers proudly with a smile."

"How many students go there?"

"I'm not sure," she pauses, thinks for a second, and finishes her thought, "Perhaps, five thousand but too many men." Then she goes on, "Yale men," she slowly shakes her head, her thoughts have apparently lapsed into past memories, "there's nothing like them." Here, Grace recites an anti–man poem. "Yale men are quite the...." Her words and eyes for the briefest moment make it clear that she's been hurt by men, as unmistakably clear as anything I've ever seen.

"Did you go to Women's Medical University in Camden? There aren't any men there," wryly I remark after she finishes.

"No," her affect more controlled, "I went right here at University."

As our conversation continues I'm very curious if she is real or playing a "Sarah Bernhardt" role. After all, life has its many villains, distressed damsels and, yes, heroes; life has its therapists and patients, and all these roles can be acted well! My request is for authenticity not dissimulation. Nevertheless, if this is an act, it's the most brilliantly awesome and convincing performance I've ever seen.

It's been a good session because my anxiety has not interfered with my ability to enjoy a light, sociable dialogue. Later in the session I tell Grace that my grandmother will be 100 years old, and I must attend a stressful family celebration. "Strife awaits me at the hand of several close relatives," I say feeling an increasing anxiety because of this less friendly subject, "especially from an overpowering, verbally abusive father and manipulative mother," and "there are OCD travel stresses, too...."

In an overt attempt at humor I say, laughing, "Could you give me a few 'party' tranquilizers?"

"Your laughter is incongruent and therefore inappropriate in therapy," Grace warns me. Her tone is friendly but authoritative. "How many do you want?" she then asks.

"Just a few," I reply passively. She writes out the prescription, and I gingerly take it between two fingers.

As I am leaving her office, I hear her remark almost casually, "I'm not going to battle with you every week!" Her innuendo that I am argumentative and insensitive seems uncalled for and has come unexpectedly. Why would she, I reflect shrugging my shoulders outside her office, make such an out of context remark especially at the session's end? And battle about what?

Nevertheless, my OCD anxiety refocuses me as I walk down the hall. There are hospital and travel fears lurking ahead. Beth meets me in the lobby and leads me to the safety of our home.

No record sent

Tuesday, Beth brings me poetry books from the library. Reading poetry provides an avenue to my emotions, not surprisingly, I relate to poets who led troubled lives, Edgar Allen Poe and Emily Dickinson. A succinct and powerful poem by Emily Dickinson catches my eye and captures my imagination: "And something odd–within//That person that I was//And this One–do not feel the same//Could it be Madness–this." Can a person, I reflect, have personality segments living in conflict? A disturbing question that is best left, restless, within me.

Later in the week Beth and I watch an intriguing movie, *The Secret Garden*. The movie is based on Frances Hodgson Burnet's book. An undercurrent of emotional complexity creates an especially compelling story, especially given my circumstances. A boy, Colin, is sealed in a world of infirmity, until, a remarkable little girl, his cousin Mary, encourages him to venture forth and experience life. I think of the "Colin" in me as I hear their tearful dialogue:

"Do you want to live?" asks Mary.

Cross and tired, Colin answers, "No. But I don't want to die. When I feel ill I lie here and think about it until I cry, and cry, and cry.... I dare say," he answers. "Let's talk about that garden."

I reflect on my OCD years gone by, years of obsessional, phobic, and depressive behaviors, the amount of tears shed and the scant tears shed for me, except by Beth. My very soul aches. But Colin's story ends favorably and so must mine! I resolve to cultivate my own garden and build my own garden path. But how? My thoughts drift to Mary and the role she plays. She may be Colin's facilitator, but it is he who demands a wheelchair to enter life. Ultimately, Colin heals himself, and I must do the same.

The scenes in which Colin and Mary talk passively contrast the scene where they start, with great energy, for the garden; I've been passive too long! How I long to be on the path, the right path, leading to my own "Garden." Don't we all have such a place in mind?

Getting there won't be very easy, like Colin, I need cultivating. And like Colin I need to find a facilitator who will give me inspiration by bringing out emotion. Beth is my love but our oneness won't force change in me: maybe Grace?

As the week passes I choose a path: to walk around the hospital, go to the library, and to the bookstore. I am elated after formulating my recovery plan, and Beth encourages me forward.

By Thursday, however, I realize there must be more to my plan. But what? Perhaps, there should be a focus on my earlier idea which lays restlessly and distractingly within me: "That person that I was//And this One//do not feel the same." My own formulation follows: "This" is the neurotic part of myself, unsure and frightened, a powerful remnant from childhood trauma and fear conditioning. "That," the adult self, is the sure and confident part of myself which is also an earlier childhood carryover.

My OCD will never go away until my mind restructures itself, so I believe. Maybe the only way to accomplish this is to disrupt my cognitively controlled, logical mind—split it into personality segments and take it into the illogic of emotional chaos: a dynamic process of madness and wellness. And so I go between the two behavioral poles of cognitive control and emotional chaos and think about "that" me (adult self) and "this" me (child/adolescent self).

"This" growls, "You cretin, you oaf, you schlemiel, it's crazy thinking; stop it!"

However, a softer and more peaceful "that" says, "'This' never let you walk your Eden." A surge of hope, of optimism, overtakes me. But my heart remembers living in a kind of Eden, in body, mind, and soul, when OCD began to tighten its viselike grip. Immediately there is self–pity; then "that" firmly speaks, "Get out of your bed!" And my answer comes, "this" the boy must reconcile with "that" my peaceful man so they can live in Eden without OCD. It is time for "this" and "that" to be integrated.

"What in the world are you thinking?!" the faithless, insecure "this" screams. "Go on your path and take your tentative steps and your giant steps with Grace. But whatever you do won't matter, your OCD, phobias, and depression will find you!" "That" then whispers and speaks again, "Nothing can bring you peace but yourself." As Emerson said: "Self reliance is the basis for human growth and dignity."

Later in the week I search for emotional inspiration, and it arrives from an unlikely source, the PBS video series, *Ken Burns' The Civil War*. A Union soldier, Sullivan Ballou's touching words are read. These words create emotion and capture my imagination. Can the integrated "this" and "that" script such soulful words to another...?

"....Sara, my love for you is deathless. It seems to bind me like mighty cables that nothing but omnipotence can break. A memory of all the blissful moments I've enjoyed with you come crowding over me, and I feel most deeply grateful to God and you that I've enjoyed them for so long, and how hard it will be for me to give them up and burn to ashes the hopes of future years. When, God willing we might still have lived and loved together and seen our boys grow up to honorable manhood around us. If I don't return, my dear Sara, never forget how much I loved you, and when my last breath escapes me on the battlefield it whispers your name. Forgive my many faults and the many pains I've caused you. How thoughtless, how foolish, I've sometimes been. But 'Oh Sara' if the dead can come back to this earth and flit unseen around those they love, I shall always be with you in the brightest day and darkest night, always, always, and when the soft breeze fans your cheek, it shall be my breath, or the cool air at your

throbbing temple, it shall be my spirit passing by."
Like so many, Sullivan Ballou died in battle.

By now, I've logged 100 hours reading poetry, watched the Civil War series for inspiration, and planned my OCD improvement strategy. Therapy has become my "daily work." My plan is complete—to encourage Grace to be my "Mary" or facilitator. For my part, I will make my hospital rounds, expose myself to OCD fears outside the hospital, and maneuver myself through submerged mental structures by journal writing.

Will Grace support me in these tentative steps back into the world? Can I take the final step, a giant stride, by myself? Will my attempt lead to therapeutic madness? or will it lead to Eden? a place free of OCD. Much, it seems, remains to be seen!

To show Grace how desperately I want to get better, I shave my long beard of 15 years. At the hospital, I transport myself, unaccompanied, with journal in hand, from the lobby to psychiatry. Once there I, proudly but nervously, sit in a chair for the first time and await Grace's arrival.

CHAPTER 3

Session 6/27

Grace, wearing a long, brown flowered dress, greets me with a personable affect. Interestingly, however, she doesn't inquire about Beth's absence. In her office we exchange a few pleasantries.

"Did you have a good week?" I question, steadying my ill at ease voice.

"No, horrible," she leans slightly in her chair, "my back is killing me. For weeks I've been lugging water from the swamp next to my house."

"Why?"

"My well's almost dry, and my garden needs to be watered."

"Why don't you buy a $20 water pump and a hose?"

"Sounds like a good idea," she answers, "I'll think about it."

I introduce my plan by saying in a timid tone, "Will you read my journal?"

"I'll be glad to," Grace replies amicably, smiling, "and make comments." Her reaction is important so my look stays with her. Time stops as she reads it.

When finished she remarks, "I can't make any comment," and leans forward in her chair. Presently she continues, "Your journal writings are powerful, and I don't want to trivialize them." I feel proud that she praises them, confused that she can't superficially comment on them, and unhappy that my plan has been placed on hold. Again, she keeps concealing her own mind and confusing mine.

"Why can't my therapist make a decision and unconfuse me?" I muse, feeling a need for closure. Grace tells me about her husband and personal life, and I tell her about Beth....

There is a long instant of dead silence; then I, with no forethought, say boldly, "I want to express feelings to a man."

"Is this man someone you know or a stranger?" Grace

hurriedly asks.

"Of course," startled by her peculiar question, I react with a defensive tone, "it's someone I know!" As I reflect on what she is implying, loneliness and remorse are felt leading me to say, "I withdrew from a friend, Gary, when I got OCD. Gary took me, a Christian, into his Jewish life and treated me like a close brother. We played tennis, socialized, and attended basketball games together." Guilt feelings surge. I'm suddenly confused, and for a moment, my OCD tensile strength of balance is absent. Fortunately, Grace's silence at my finish tells me it is time to regroup and move on.

As the session unfolds another aberrant remark occurs, and, for no reason at all, I say, "Grace, I'm afraid of women." My nerves are now twitching as my sheath of impermeability has completely collapsed.

She seems intrigued and quickly asks, "Why are you afraid of women?"

"Rejection!" I bellow, reacting without intention and instantly feeling vulnerable.

"I might unknowingly reject you," Grace asserts with conviction, "but if I do happen to reject you it will be unintentional even if it is unknowingly done." While her words have left me confused, their intent is understood.

Frightfully my hand touches the doorknob. I am committed to healing. The session suddenly ends without her mentioning Beth's absence or my shaved beard. Walking down the corridor I worry that therapy is becoming an instrument for exploring—mournful and never–ending remembrances.

Session 6/27 One hour psychiatric therapy

"I've been doing my homework," Patient brought in a lengthy, passionate journal regarding desire for cure versus fear of change. Expressed determination to begin exposure—would like to spend part of sessions exploring hospital. Continues ambivalent regarding medications.

O: Unshaven, **(Shaved)** full affect. Took appointment card, opened doors himself. A/P: Patient beginning exposure therapy; very motivated. Will visit hospital library next appointment with patient. RTC one week.

By the time Beth greets me in the lobby, my focus has changed to OCD. Two self–imposed OCD challenges await me. First, I shop in a crowded supermarket, and my hand places groceries into a shopping cart. Afterward, a more stressful event unfolds: I stop at a store where Beth will purchase garden shoes for me. To most people buying shoes is easy, but not for someone with OCD. My shoes are usually purchased through a mail order catalogue, and if they look "tried on" Beth returns them. But no matter where the shoes are purchased, they will not be worn for several weeks: this is my decontamination process.

Entering the store is to be the only OCD challenge, so I believe. But, then, after selecting a pair of shoes the salesperson says, "Try them on!"

Another challenge—no way I think and reply assertively, "Don't need to! They will fit fine! Just hand them to my wife and she'll buy them!" The poison hemlock is avoided.

"Try them on!!" The clerk ignores my words and places the shoes on the floor and again says firmly, "You must try them on!" Then something wonderful happens; my foot feels the kind touch of a strange shoe. Maybe these are only baby steps to most, but to me they are "giant steps," steps not taken in many, many years. As we drive home I feel elated by today's accomplishments.

The next morning I write, abstractly, to cope with my anxiety and to distance myself from disruptive feelings, but paradoxically the things I write about bring up feelings. Nevertheless, there is a certain allure to this process, even though my anxiety level may go from bad to worse....

To ask "why" is to speak of the way one poor soul loses his way, wandering in a circle, creating a maelstrom of idleness, loneliness, and stress: all linked by two seemingly antithetical tangents—self–motivation and avoidance. I lost my drive for self–motivation and avoided things both pleasant and unpleasant. Focusing my idle energy on the perceived threat of catching AIDS led me into darkness. Now I search for that point of light to lead me out. Nothing, it seems, will ever take away this anguish: ten years of life is wasted, never to return. Anguish stings my soul.... After awhile I commit the ultimate weakness; I stop writing and fall asleep.

As the week progresses, I realize that powerful motivators and a structured plan are still necessary. Trying on shoes represents healing progress, but it is only a mere step forward. Charging myself through symbolic writing may create this motivation. Finding the symbol isn't difficult. I was born at the end of the WWII, and my wife served twenty two years in the United States military. Throughout this period I visited war monuments: Verdun, Gettysburg, Valley Forge; during the Vietnam War I was in Southeast Asia. I metaphorically think of OCD as my enemy and the quest to get better as a "war." And so I write about my battle strategy.

The fight for healing has started with encouraging victories but these are only altercations. "Who is the enemy?" the soldier in me inquires. The general already posted in my mind answers, "OCD anxiety." My soldier's soul is frightened because this enemy tortured, despoiled, and imprisoned him ten years before. Its Corps are mighty fighters and their names are quite well known: apprehension, tension, self–doubt, disquietude; and without doubt, the most feared of all, "relentlessness."

My general identifies our Corps and finds: Beth's endless love, Grace, my tenacity, and the most effectual, faith in God. He evaluates each Corp for he lost one war and understands the ugliness of battle. My general knows that Beth will fight and help the wounded, that my tenacity will stand it's ground, and that faith can carry any day. The Grace Corp is, however, indecisive and untried. The battle plan is complete. A plan predicated on no compromise, to fight and fight and fight until victorious, for there shall be no retreat!

My real life strategy is unadorned: When I encounter an

anxiety–producing threat, then, I will immediately expose myself to a higher level threat. In ascending order such threats are: tying my shoes, putting groceries in kitchen cabinets, eating in a restaurant, and shaking someone's hand. This soldier and his general recognize the plan's peril. Our OCD foe is sure and staunch, well entrenched, and knows me better than I know it. Be that as it may, I promise myself that this is not to be my Verdun, that my body will not lie in a metaphorical Flander's Field. (McCrae)

> In Flander's field the poppies blow
> Between the crosses, row by row,
> That mark our place; and in the sky
> The larks, still bravely singing, fly
> Scarce heard amid the guns below.
> We are the Dead, Short days ago
> We lived, felt Dawn, saw sunset glow,
> Loved and were loved, and we lie
> In Flander's field.

"This" and "that" speak to me with opposing voices.

"Oh! You'll catch AIDS," "this" says to me, but "that" knows it isn't true.

"It's just a game or folly," "this" says to me, but "that" knows it isn't true.

"Just try again if you fail," "that" says to me, but I know this is my last chance.

"Beth and Grace will fail you," "this" says to me, but "that" knows it won't be true. There's no one else to blame but me.

In a darker moment of self–doubt and to seek more feeling, I write: It brings me sorrow and pain to write these words about myself, for in many ways I have been blessed with talent but am crippled by failure. My soul is sad because a precious life from God has been wasted. I cry and pray, steeling myself for the coming battle to heal myself. How I wish it would be an actual battle! A soldier walks, as commanded, into harm's way, but if he survives he walks away. Conversely, this soldier fights an enemy from within. There is no refuge from my enemy, except perchance, a dreamless sleep.

KEY TO VICTORY: To lead "this" out of OCD darkness through my faith in God, love for Beth, and Grace's guidance. The past is forever dead, so I open life's door and step toward the unknown.

That afternoon, Beth and I take a walk. We only discuss therapy and both agree that my journal writings are complex, abstract, and emotionally charged. "Perhaps it goes like this," Beth comments trying to make sense out of things, "your writings are bringing up unresolved feelings; then, to cope, you write. But this writing only causes these feelings to get stronger, and so on...."

"You're right. It sure seems like my writings are bringing up a lot of unexplained feelings. I just wish these feelings would go away." I then tell Beth how this cycle is influencing my therapy behavior. "When I described my relationship with Gary to Grace, I felt exceptional guilt and remorse and didn't even tell Grace I called him several years later, apologized, and we had a pleasant chat."

"You're certainly expressing yourself differently now that your writings have elicited these strong feelings," adds Beth. Immediately she continues, "Maybe your mind is sorting through your unresolved feelings at a subconscious level."

"How right you are," I answer. "My story about Gary illustrates how feelings about relationships are magnified in a therapeutic setting." Our eyes meet. "Disturbing but true," we, perhaps, think in unison.

Session 7/06

I sit in the unusually crowded psychiatric reception area and anxiously await Grace. Her arrival and smile are welcome sights. She escorts me to a conference room waiting for me to open doors as we go. I nervously comply while wondering if an AIDS infected person has previously touched them. Upon our arrival, she tells me proudly, "We're meeting here today because my office–mate is doing record keeping on his day off. Isn't he dedicated!" Then she continues, smiling, "We're going to visit the hospital library today after we talk for awhile."

"I'm looking forward to going," I remark while handing her my journal. I review it for twenty minutes, after which, we are off to the library. As we saunter along the corridor I notice how she hugs my shoulder. Her closeness has a settling effect on me. We chat pleasantly.

"There's nothing like living in the country," Grace remarks. Then she goes on to say, "I love it and could never live in the city."

"Why?"

"There are too many people in the city," her voice rings with resoluteness. "In the country I can take long walks and be alone with nature...!" Grace tells me she is a vegetarian, loves to cook, and about her husband's deformed fingers. In the library she shows me a resource computer and how to operate its data bank. We play with the computer like a couple of kids. She smiles as we play, stands uncomfortably close, and says, softening her voice, "You're a very intelligent and creative guy."

"Thanks," I reply. Her flattery feels good. Although our library conversation is "casual," she appears nervous. Under my camouflaged OCD demeanor, there is nervousness, too. The stress of touching door knobs and computer keys is causing it. Nothing is going to calm me.

"You have quite a bit of philosopher in you," she candidly comments as we leave the library; adding, "You're very talented!"

"I suspect my obsessive mind has made me appear like a philosopher," I respond as my ego rises and good feelings set in. "Next week, I'm going to write a philosophical narrative about my OCD illness." Grace makes no comment and redirects the conversation to herself.

Later we chat in her office, which has become available.

Unexpectedly Grace says, "I want you to be aware that your 'Christian teachings' prevent you from taking medication."

"Not really!" I quickly, firmly respond while reflecting a hint of shock at her insinuation that God is working against me, and that HE is making me do harmful things to myself.

"That's probably what's happening," she resolutely replies, smiling, "and I want to let you know again your 'Christian teachings' are doing it...." Her bold caricature of a Christian causes me to inquire about her beliefs.

"Grace, what are your beliefs?" cautiously I ask.

"I'm an atheist like many psychiatrists," she confidently answers.

"How about your family's beliefs?"

"My husband was some kind of Catholic, but now, like me, he doesn't have an interest in religion. My parents," she continues, her affect detached, "were both atheists. Like them, I don't believe there is a God...."

What a great discussion to continue: God's power to heal the mind. Unfortunately, the session is almost over. "Perhaps, another day," I tell myself. The telephone rings; her next appointment has arrived.

Quickly, I ask her to call me "John." She doesn't answer right away; then she smiles and with a raised eyebrow replies, "I don't call other patients by name, but in your case I'll make a very special exception." Her comment about how she treats other patients confuses me and seems rude. Nevertheless, instinct and experience tell me that a little tender persuasion will change her dehumanizing methodology.

Session 7/6 One and one–quarter hour psychotherapy

Exposure therapy to begin–45 minute walk to library, use of consumer computer there by patient. Patient toured the stacks, opened all doors, shook hands at end of visit (his initiative) Anxiety 30/100 at beginning of session 50/100 at peak in library. No behavioral abnormalities noted. O: Clean shaven, good eye contact negative for psycho–motor agitation. mood good, affect full, slightly distracted, frequent humor. A/P: Patient continuing to work–has begun exposure successfully. Will go to store in mall next week to continue exposure. If patient has not spontaneously begun homework by then, I will encourage that—my guess is that he'll initiate it. No medications **(Mistake—gave me medication on 6/13)** Patient tolerating exposure without them and requests continuing.

On our journey home, as usual, I focus on my OCD. My mood is quite upbeat, so Beth and I shop, uneventfully, at a supermarket. The checkout line is long, so I return alone to our car. Here I notice a young boy taking his dog for a walk. He waves after noticing our dog, and I wave back while thinking, "It would be fun to talk with him about dogs." Wanting to talk to a stranger is unusual behavior for me. Good feelings have emerged—ones not often felt.

CHAPTER 4

To what extent do unknown longings contribute to my Obsessive Compulsive Disorder? As Saint Exupéry said, "Only the unknown frightens men. But once a man has faced the unknown, that terror becomes the known." My mind seems open to probing.

Psychological Transference

In the next session I enter psychological transference with Grace. Transference is a patient's overdeveloped affection and attachment to his or her therapist which can only be traced to the patient's prior unconscious, wishful fantasies about significant others in their life. Transference behavior is emotionally driven and capricious: feelings are magnified, whimsical, impulsive, unpredictable, and addictive. Think of transference in this way:

Beth and I had a dog, Penny, who "disliked" mail carriers. Our otherwise "friendly" dog would bark and growl at their sight. We knew the reason for Penny's behavior: in puppyhood a mail carrier hit her several times with his bag. Subsequent carriers were assorted sizes, sexes, didn't always carry bags, wore different uniforms, and weren't aggressive toward her. But fifteen years and twenty mail carriers later, our Penny was still growling at most, but not *all* of them. When Penny barked and growled at a carrier, even when away from the house, did she bring up unresolved puppy feelings? Her behavior was certainly magnified and impulsive.

Session 7/13

When Grace and I return to her office after visiting the bookstore, I feel anxious and distracted. I suspect exposure to OCD fears has caused this, after all, handling books and money may have frightened me. She asks me to score my anxiety "now" on a graduated scale of one to a hundred. I tell her about my OCD improvement.... The session ends.

Session 7/13 One and one–half hour psychotherapy

Visit to bookstore, patient handling money, books, doors and coming in close proximity to others without hand washing. Has been out shopping for groceries and shoes with wife. Anxiety today peaked–40/100. O: Clean shaven, wearing wedding ring. **(Last session too)** Cooperative and pleasant. Affect full, congruent, minimal anxiety. A/P: Continued progress; patient independently initiated homework and will continue. Will begin to formulate a plan with patient for social exposure, while continuing up the hierarchy of intra–hospital exposure. Level of functioning outside therapy is increasing to allow shopping with wife.

As we reenter the story, the hospital bookstore visit with Grace during therapy is finished. That evening inexplicable emotions drive my writing. When I finish writing, cognitive and emotional confusion reign.

Session 7/13 The Book Store Visit

A trip to buy a book is scary to a kid like me. Mommy told me last week we were going next Thursday. I don't think too far ahead at my age. Wednesday I started to get scared and could not sleep all night. It ain't that I'm scared of the bookstore, but I don't know what it is, I think I got nightmares but don't remember. I like spending time with Mommy and she is good to me. She likes to play games with me, but she wants me to grow up and that's hard for a kid like me. It's time to go and I'm scared, boy it ain't easy trying to be a big boy. I'm really afraid now, maybe she will not mind if I hold her hand—it will not work—Mommy will tell me to act like a big boy. Mommy's got a real loose dress, maybe I can just hang on. Mommy will not like that either so I'll just stay close. I ain't going to get lost.

Wow, look at all these books, but there are no kids like me here. Everybody is old, I think I'll move a little closer to Mommy. You think Mommy thinks I'm scared. I must keep thinking big boys don't cry, boy would Mommy be mad cause she's doin' it for me. But maybe I should be a little kid forever, it sure is easier. But Mommy knows best. That book looks good.... And we're going. But Mommy says, "Let's look at this book." Wow, we ain't leaving so I better keep close. You mean I gotta pay for the book? Now I'm really scared and I think I did not count my change. It ain't easy to take a kid like me to buy a book, and teach him to be a big boy. I ain't going to tell her how scared I am because maybe she will not like me anymore. I don't think Mommy likes me writing stories to her, "cause big guys don't write, they talk to their Mommy, but I'm kinda scared to talk to her." I don't want to make her scared like me.

This bookstore writing creates a nasty, emotion–charged night and day for me! The description of the boy grabbing his mother's skirt is symbolic, no doubt, but of whom? Did Grace represent Beth, or my mother, or someone else? After considerable thinking, I make an interpretation: the bookstore description is about my childish feelings toward my mother. Grace, a thirtyish psychiatrist, has become a mother image to me, a fifty year old man.

What has caused this? As we walked along the hospital corridor, she talked about her son "Phil" and how much she cared for him. Her expressions evoked potent feelings of jealousy as she stood close to me in the bookstore and continued to describe "Phil." When she seemed disinterested in a book I handed her, I sensed rejection. By the time we headed back, I felt painfully rejected. How arduous it was for me to touch a book, touch money, pay a cashier, and receive change, and Grace had made no comment about me trying to get better!

CHAPTER 5

Today, my bewildered frame of mind continues. To cope, I write about therapy and my childhood, eventually, my thinking drifts to a friend of many years ago.

Twenty–three years ago Ruth shared with me her deepest emotional feelings. I remember it like yesterday. Our relationship was clearly defined by tender feelings. A beautiful Japanese woman and Haole man met at work on the enchanted island of Oahu, and together we shared the sensitivities of our separate lives. Ruth was an empathetic and delightful person; slowly we grew closer. One day, while we were casually walking along a street in Honolulu, she turned toward me timidly and said, "John, my husband doesn't satisfy me in bed." Her disclosure caught me by surprise and presented a disturbing consequence, so I, "kinda," glossed over it. Our relationship was never the same.

"This" and "that," have their individual words to say. "This" callously says, "You feel bad because you passed up a good chance," but "that" knows the truth. Ruth was a shy, sensitive woman who expressed a personal concern which I ignored. Our story is painful to relive and a question remains: What do all these confused feelings toward Ruth mean? With no resolution in sight, I think about my OCD progress.

Now in its fourth week, my attack on OCD continues as Beth and I shop. Shopping forces me to open doors and mingle with strangers. For the first time in many years, I look at strangers without wondering if they are AIDS carriers. I have eaten berries from a bush, and toast in the morning with my hands, and best of all, I felt a greasy hamburger bun between my fingers. Another example of my successful attack: We ate dinner at a friend's home who had had a blood transfusion. After dinner he rudely flossed his teeth as we talked. He, then, touched me and I didn't obsess, too much.

The strategy to challenge myself with more powerful AIDS related stimuli, such as shaking hands with a friend, when I'm anxious about a lower stimulus such as touching my dog, is working. I am fighting my way back into life; my quality of life is improving. Beth is delighted and I am inspired—my heart just feels good.

Beth and I dance for hours in our living room on Saturday evening concluding the most emotionally disconcerting week of my life. How incongruent are my current behaviors: I uncharacteristically dance with my wife, sentimentally revisit Ruth, and emotionally attach to my therapist. Wow! What a tangled web. All of my feelings are toward women, but, yet, I am afraid of them because I fear their rejection. Grace must help me untangle this web. Nervous, worrying, I hardly slept last night, but heading toward therapy I feel fresh and alert.

Session 7/20 My Twilight Zone

Grace is prompt and greets me with a smile that instantly evokes attachment feelings. I rise and off we go. Here I am, a fifty–year old man with intense love emotions toward my young therapist, someone vaguely known. For no external reason, she is intimidating me. How inane I feel as we enter her office.

"Grace," I say timidly as we sit, my pulse rising, "I've these strange feelings toward you, and I wrote this weird story about you being my mother."

"What kind of feelings do you have for me?" she swiftly asks. Her look has changed quickly from subdued to excited.

"It's hard to explain," I pause feeling unsure of how to phrase my words, "but I felt a lot of emotion when you stood close to me in the bookstore, and the emotion seemed to intensify when you talked about Phil, your son...."

"Of course," Grace remarks, as if I've answered a test question correctly, "I know exactly what happened. You felt jealous when I talked about Phil. That's definitely it," she seems to be talking more to herself than me. Swiftly, Grace asks to see my journal and reads it keenly, as I sit silently with an analytical eye on her.

"I'm sure of it!" she says emphatically, placing my journal on her desk. "You're in transference with me!" "What's transference?" passively I ask.

"Transference," she answers displaying an atypical decisiveness, "happens when you place your feelings for others onto me. You can project feelings about your mother, father, friend, wife, or anybody onto me. Transference is an important healing concept in therapy!"

Perhaps for no other reason than wanting to escape unsettled feelings, I inquire when she pauses, "Where are we going today?"

"We aren't going anywhere," Grace firmly replies, peering with a hint of disapproval at me. "It's more important that we stay here and talk." My expression instantly dissolves into one of disappointment, but, still, her discourse returns to transference. "You'll express your innermost feelings to me," she continues, "and you'll say things that you wouldn't tell anyone but me...."

"Am I now given a therapeutic role," I think as she speaks, "where I'm required to express imprudent thoughts to her? Is she trying to bring back the sorrow and anger of the past? What healing value is there in this?" A quagmire of confusion encapsulates me. I know I ought to ask questions, but at this emotional time it seems impossible.

Grace asserts, "Future therapy sessions will be conducted in my office."

After an hour she stands, smiling, and says, "We are going to meet one hour this week, not our usual one and a half hours, and we will meet one hour next week, and I may reduce future session time to forty–five minutes or, perhaps, a half–hour." As these words leave her mouth, childish feelings of rejection overcome me just as in the bookstore.

With a disappointed look—my eyes turn from hers and my head droops as I say, "You're not being fair with me. We agreed to longer meetings. It's not fair!" My voice is unsteady; my words are guarded.

Grace answers over her shoulder as she leads me to the

door, "A time change is appropriate because transference is intense."

When I leave Grace is standing unusually close to me. Her eyes mirror mine. Nothing that is happening seems to have reality, and in a state of blurred confusion I want to hold her, though I want her to hold me more. In the corridor these emotions settle. "Where am I heading?" I ask myself as I walk down the hallway to meet Beth.

Session 7/20 One hour psychotherapy

Patient has been continuing with homework–shopping with wife, visited a friend whose special problem is friend's blood transfusion; plans a game of tennis with wife today. Minimal anxiety regarding OCD symptoms. Concern regarding increased high anxiety around memories of his mothers emotional neglect following his sibling's birth at age seven, stimulated by transferential feelings toward me. Discussed transference and boundaries. (Patient was able, before this meeting to resolve his own anxiety and appreciate the transferential nature of his experience).O: Clean–shaven, appropriate dress, handled door-knobs. Affect full, congruent. A/P Progressing in Cognitive Behavioral therapy, Dynamic issue has emerged, patient stable but with some anxiety and decreased function **(not true)** earlier in week. Will approach boundaries with caution. Return to clinic in one week.

After therapy Beth and I play tennis on the university courts. This activity is part of my self–imposed OCD challenge. Repeatedly hitting tennis balls keeps me from thinking about therapy, but the activity offers only a short respite.

I once said to Grace, "Someone should hit me over the head and rearrange my brain cells." Now, transference is doing exactly that. Transference thoughts are so palpably different that it may be possible for me to explore childhood emotions and memories; here in this twilight zone, it seems, anything can happen. The day ends as Beth and I, feeling young and alive, dance the night away.

The next night I am restless; I rise at 3 A.M. and write to cope. A deep well of emotion directs my writing. Thoughts of my childhood take me out of the OCD inferno in which I've been serving my time: But only to the tormented parts of my childhood which if left unresolved will disrupt me forever. Childhood hurts are felt and tears sting my eyes as I write about my family.

Form birth to five years of age, I lived with my parents, grandparents, an aunt, uncle, and two cousins. We lived in a tiny duplex that had three bedrooms and only one bathroom. This was my grandparents' loving home. Five men were influential in my early life. My maternal grandfather was by nature a quiet man, yet, he showed an intense interest in me and a loving bond existed between us. Holding his hand as he lay dying, I felt the strength of his love. My paternal grandfather died when I was five, and my memories of him, though vague, are also loving. Two uncles were affectionate toward me. My father was self–centered, often argumentative, verbally abusive, and uncaring about others' feelings. Four women were pivotal in my childhood: two grandmothers, an aunt, and mother. I left childhood with love feelings toward my mother that were camouflaged under feelings of rejection, anger, and abandonment. She was emotionally immature, insecure, and rarely displayed any empathetic feelings toward me. The love bonds with the other women are more clearly defined.

After moving from my grandparents' home at age six, there is an image of me as a child lying in bed crying. I was distraught because my mother and father were fighting endlessly, all night, night after night. Powerlessness and hopelessness consumed me because I couldn't help my mother, and I cried in prayer for her and for me: "God, I'm just a little kid. Please help me know what to do. Help me, please," prayed a tearful I. Nevertheless, the screaming between my mother and father never ended even though I cried, fearfully, in my mother's arms. Finally one night there were no more tears and prayers for help. These tears are rare.

Oh, how I tried to change my situation by running for help to my grandmother's home. My father and mother were never abusive there. Grandmother loved me, and there was safety in her home.

"Grandmother," I cried tearfully, "my father hates me, and they scream at each other all night, every night."

"Your parents love you, that's the way your father is, and it's hard for your mother to deal with him," she always said.

"But Grandma! You don't know how scared it makes me," cried I, louder.

"Your parents love you!" she firmly repeated. "Here, have some ice cream, and you'll feel better."

One day I stopped telling her because she wasn't going to help me. Yet, I only wanted my parents to behave in a loving manner toward each other and me.

My brother was born when I was six years old. On the way home from the hospital, my hand was extended to touch him. "Don't touch his head! You'll kill him!" my father screamed uncontrollably. To this day the trauma remains. Unexpectedly one day, my parents withdrew me from a church school and enrolled me in a public school. Everyday I ran away from there and wandered the city streets heading for "nowhere," trying to "escape" my feelings of rejection and loneliness. An assortment of benevolent people found me and took me home.

One day my Uncle Dan caught me. I resisted his effort to take me home by holding onto a fire hydrant. "Leave me alone! Don't take me home!!!" was my scream as a crowd gathered around us. That evening my father threatened to dress me like a girl and walk me around the school yard. I surrendered fearing ridicule from my classmates, and because I knew my home life wasn't going to change. Shortly thereafter, I came home from school and found my cat and best friend, Snoopy, missing!

Church activities and Sunday school teachings were a focal point in my early life. Still, church doctrine was difficult to apply within my feelings of rejection, loneliness, and abandonment. Questions like—If God loves me, why doesn't He make my life better? How can I keep forgiving people who hurt me night after night?—were asked, but practical doctrine was never found.

Even today I ask myself these questions. And I know there's a part of me that's still angry at God because He didn't help me as a child. Therefore, I decide to learn more about the way of the Lord and ask Beth to call a pastor.

Beth telephones a Baptist minister at a small church in Lancaster and explains my OCD and our need for spiritual guidance. He gives us an appointment. I am anxious and troubled as we approach the church. Memories from long ago have surfaced: my family's criticism of church leaders and the special interest groups who used the Bible to justify their personal and political agendas.

On a more positive side, there were numerous pleasant social and spiritual memories during these years. With such a mix of memories, I often think that organized religion confuses many people and turns more souls away from God than toward Him.

The pastor, Kenneth Paul, is a man who represents God to others. For half an hour I explain my need for spiritual guidance, assuring him that psychiatry takes care of my therapeutic needs. My outward demeanor is one of slight nervousness, but internally there is much anxiety for God represents a powerful figure.

"Sorry I can't help you," he says, "but you're welcome to attend church here." He stands, a sign the meeting is over, and proceeds, "Before you leave let me say a prayer with you both."

"We don't need therapy just spiritual guidance!" Beth desperately insists again.

"Let me give you the names of several religiously oriented counselors if you insist. I don't know how much they charge, but they can provide spiritual guidance for you both." He gives us their names. After which he prays for us. All the way home Beth cries.

I try to comfort her with this thought, the church isn't God and all pastors, unfortunately, aren't representatives of God. "He didn't want to be bothered with us," I conclude while also feeling rejected.

The next day Beth tries again. She calls another pastor and explains our need for spiritual guidance, "I'm sorry," this pastor replies, "but I'm a busy interim pastor and you should go to a pastoral counselor for spiritual guidance." As Beth hangs up tears flow again. However, I am resolute and say while also feeling forsaken, "I'm not paying to find God; let's move on.... We'll find God ourselves." We decide, therefore, to change direction and that brings my thinking back to therapy.

A strange current of emotion flows through my thoughts today: I don't know whether I am, truly, attracted or repelled by Grace—only that she deeply moves me.

For some reason Grace has asked me to call her today.

"How has your week been?" asks Grace.

"I have many indistinguishable feelings which I'm trying to decipher through writing," I answer.

"Don't worry about them," Grace says encouragingly. "It's quite normal to have confused feelings when you're in transference." Quickly she adds, "You must be functioning to go through therapy...." Her comment dumbfounds me as I stare out the window and think: "I'm already in therapy, and she knows my life has been improving!"

"Goodbye." And she is gone. Great conversation, I think blankly.

Explaining to Grace how an OCD controlled mind functions directs my writing. Several weeks ago I wrote that my fight against OCD would not end like Verdun, the infamous WWI battle. A few years ago I grimly pondered its massive battlefield and graveyard and thought about that waste of human life. Called by some the greatest human tragedy of the twentieth century—that battle exacted six hundred thousand casualties.... Symbolism like this emotionally stimulates me to fight against OCD. My mind is skillful and tireless and with it a detailed house can be constructed.... Riddles, mental games, and competition stimulate it. There, logical and rational constructs such as "this" and "that" are resourcefully created.... Complex structure is essential here, although it may be antithetical to therapy which appears to be ambiguous and elementary.

CHAPTER 6

After writing all day, I am sitting in the living room thinking about therapy. Slowly I turn to Beth and say, my voice low but clear, "How strange! I believe I can walk anywhere in the hospital, to the intensive care unit or anywhere. It feels like my OCD fears are gone."

"Are you sure?!" Beth hesitates, her look becoming surprised.

"Let me find a powerful fear to show you it's possible, something right here in the house," boldly I reply. After a long moment of thought I touch Beth's blood. This is a compelling moment for us and the most effectual OCD challenge so far. I pray thanking God and asking for His continued help. Beth feeling blessed also prays silently. As I pray an energy surges through me, and the presence of God is felt. God is with me and has given me the strength to overcome OCD. The experience lasts a few seconds. Then with tearful eyes I speak to Beth, "God is with me, and I understand the kind of love that I must hold for my parents—God doesn't expect me to accept their damaging behavior, but He does expect me to pray for their souls and repentance."

Until now, Beth and I never truly understood how a spiritual experience healed and guided others. My direction is clear. University hospital is the ideal place to face my HIV (AIDS) fear. Grace wants to stay in her office tomorrow, but I am going to show her I can travel through that hospital and successfully confront fear, after fear, after fear!!!

Session 7/27

I arrive early for my appointment. While reaching for a magazine, frightfully, I almost touch a red, gooey, blood like spot on its cover: a sign, no doubt, of what lies ahead. Grace arrives, and I point to the spot. Only days ago I would have become obsessional and asked for reassurance: today neither occurs. She apathetically looks at the spot.

"Grace," I say excitedly as we enter her office, "I want to challenge my OCD by walking through the hospital."

"No!" she swiftly asserts shaking her head and appearing somewhat annoyed at my suggestion. "It's more important we stay in my office and do therapy. I've already told you that!"

I smile and point to the door. "Let's go! I want to challenge my OCD!" This is a special day and too long in coming, so I keep insisting.

"Well...," a pause, "OK," she says reluctantly and opens the door for me.

As we begin walking, I realize the very formidable challenge ahead—plenty of blood, blood products, and many other fear stimuli. Without question, hospitals are aversive places for me. But I feel God's calming presence....

"It's difficult for me to read your anxiety level so tell me if you're getting too anxious," suggests Grace as we, shoulders hugging, walk down the main hospital corridor.

"Sure." I nod.

Her nervousness is apparent because she's opening doors for me. Grace guides me through ward after ward. We sit for awhile in the pediatric ward and then in the emergency room. Catching me by surprise, she asks, "Have you memorized all the poetry you write to me?"

"No, I have a good memory," I reply proudly, "but not that good."

Grace is uncommonly talkative today, perhaps, another sign of her anxiety. On the return trip she tells me about a wonderful man who had been her patient. A sudden shadow crosses her face, but she covers it with a smile and comments, "I liked him a lot and we had a good relationship," she lulls for a moment letting me know she is deeply feeling. "Unfortunately, he was diagnosed with terminal cancer," her voice trailing off. Then she goes on, "I felt so bad about it that I asked another physician to tell him. After which I waited twenty–four hours before I went to see him."

"Oh, I understand you did your best," I reply giving her the solace I gave my mother but internally thinking, "Grace, much like my mother, is wrapped up in her own feelings."

Upon entering her office, I feel proud and satisfied about my accomplishment. Immediately, I hand her my journal and explain my spiritual experience. I've anticipated questions like: How do you feel about your experience with God? Have you always believed in the power of God through faith to heal? Why do you think it happened to you at this time?

"Did you and Beth feel a rapture?" asks Grace.

"No, I felt the presence of God," I confidently reply.

"Did you have an out–of–body experience?"

"Grace, what's an out–of–body experience?"

"It's not important," she replies and goes on,"Did you hear voices speaking to you telling you what to do?"

"No, there were no voices telling me what to do. But the voice of God was there."

"Are you sure of that?" she asks looking at me blankly.

"Yes," I reply, realizing that only a devout atheist would question the inner voice of God. Abruptly I say, "God has given me the strength to overcome my OCD," realizing that she doesn't believe me, I become wordless. Her denial of my belief in God's healing power has annoyed me; she notices it and changes direction. In childhood I rarely challenged my mother or father when they negated my beliefs, today is no different.

Grace's agenda deals solely with transference. "My job," she commences displaying an unusual exuberance, "will be to create a new mother image for you. This," she assures me, "will be your key to healing." Grace pauses briefly, perhaps to gather her thoughts. Slowly she continues, "To this end, we'll enter your 'psychological' garden and clear out weeds. But first we have to fence the garden through no touching. If we touch our transference bond will be broken, and we won't be able to do any weeding...."

"Has she made this up?" I think ironically after she's finished, "or read about it in one of her professional books?" These changes, however, don't seem important.

Toward the session's end, Grace tells me we will only

meet for fifty minute sessions and says, "Transference can be intense for us." Like in the last session, her words elicit rejection feelings—I turn away from her gaze in childlike fashion while feeling disrupted, dominated. The session ends with me thinking, "Why can't she hold my hand and support me on occasion?"

Session 7/26 One and one–half hour psychotherapy
Patient stated he felt he was well on the way to recovery–has been shopping by himself and as a self–assigned home exposure touched his wife's menstrual blood without intense anxiety—in fact felt a tremendous joy, freedom of what he described to be a religious intensity. Today we toured inpatient units in the hospital, acting as someone would when visiting a friend–walking slowly, peering into rooms. Many IV poles, some blood visible. Minimal anxiety. Also walked through the Emergency Department and spent some time sitting in the waiting room conversing. Minimal anxiety.

Discussed initiating psychotherapy with goal of exploring 1. loneliness and 2. feelings of rejection which patient has developed unsatisfactory defenses against since about the age of seven. Discussed his transference feelings toward me as rejecting mother. Discussed boundaries–needed to formalize, given somewhat more informal style in our Cognitive Behavioral Therapy— i.e. shaking hands, chatting, longer session length.

O: Clean–shaven, good hygiene, appropriate dress. Speech normal volume and rate and prosody. Thought Process (TP) logical and coherent. (TC) thought content negative for suicidal ideation, negative for homicidal ideation negative for audio/visual hallucinations, negative for delusions. Mood hopeful, happy affect full calm congruent. A/P: Cognitive Behavioral Therapy is essentially at an end–will monitor for combination fears or for other anxiety symptoms. Patient's description of near–religious experience seems appropriate given the circumstances and on Mental Status Exam there is no histrionic or grandiose signs. Will commence dynamic psychotherapy next week planning a total of about fifteen sessions ending in about late November. Session length fifty minutes. Will explore rejection, isolation, and relationship with mother and father in general with the goal of preventing relapse into severe debilitating symptomatology, increasing functioning to possibly allow patient to return to work after a period of stability. Patient understands and agrees with goals with need to consciously maintain more formal boundaries. RTC one week. (**This note dated incorrectly for 7/26**)

Walking toward the lobby I hear the strains and remember the words, "And there proclaim, My God how great Thou art," from the wonderful hymn "How Great Thou Art." The music is uplifting—a message from God to keep me on my way. God has given me the strength to resist OCD and resist I shall.

"I'm glad you heard that hymn," Beth says happily as we meet in the lobby. "It must have been especially for you because I've never heard the pianist play a hymn."

The next morning I challenge my OCD by visiting two auto repair shops, then I visit a supermarket where the clerk sneezes into his hand, picks up the change, and hands it to me. Without obsessing I accept it. I feel confident and prepared to meet OCD adversity. But what does this have to do with "transference psychotherapy?" On the way home from the market, Beth addresses transference therapy and says, "John, you have a lot of problems dealing with your parents. Perhaps, therapy will help you work them out."

"You're right," I reply feeling more sure of a positive outcome than usual and going on to say,"Something's bound to change with all these transference feelings I have toward Grace." There's a long lull before I remark, "And through transference she's going to give me a new mother image." We both smile, quickly, our faces mirroring confusion and hope.

"You haven't had any success with your first three therapies. Maybe it will be different this time. We have to be optimistic," adds Beth encouragingly.

"No sense in repeating the same failed therapies...," I reply while drifting into silent thinking about them. Because of Beth's career moves, I've changed psychiatrists several times. Dr. Fong, my first psychiatrist, was a nationally known psychodynamic therapist and directed a residency program where Beth was a nursing administrator. He had previously worked at the Menninger Institute, which is known for a psychoanalytical approach.

Dr. Fong rarely asked a question or made a comment. In our fourth session he suggested that I focus on family problems and my AIDS fear. Since he seldom spoke his words were taken seriously. In a session he said, "Why do you take it?" after I explained how my father verbally bullied me. These words encouraged me to respond differently to my father's aggression, to meet his verbal aggression with my aggression—it happened—an aggressive verbal confrontation took place; my mother cried, Beth was upset, my father and I were angry at each other. Still, nothing changed! Fighting back hadn't helped me get better. Another time Dr. Fong said, "How can you touch tennis balls that roll across the court and not other objects on the ground?" Shortly, thereafter, I gave up tennis which was my only outside socializing activity.

Only once did I telephone him for help. My finger had been stuck by something while picking up leaves. Later that day I noticed a syringe on the ground. Seeing this syringe sent me into obsessional thinking of the worst kind....

"You'll have to deal with it until our next session," Dr. Fong said firmly, refusing to talk with me about it. "Goodbye," and he was gone.

Driven by fear, I compulsively looked for another syringe in over one hundred leaf bags. Four agonizing obsessional days of unbagging and rebagging leaves followed. Would discussing this obsession with Dr. Fong have helped? Who knows? But it couldn't have hurt because my OCD worsened over the next several years. After Beth and I were transferred to Germany, he sent a letter telling me he noticed OCD improvement. "An interesting observation Dr. Fong's made," I said to Beth after reading his letter, "I'm now housebound and much worse, but he thinks I'm getting better."

"Little does he know," Beth dejectedly commented, shrugging her shoulders and shaking her head.

In Germany I met for twenty sessions with my second

psychiatrist, Dr. Richard Gordon. Rick was more interactive than Dr. Fong but also encouraged me to speak life–irritant words or to complain about my circumstance. By the end of his therapy, my OCD symptoms had become so debilitating that Beth was forced to retire. We returned to the United States and purchased a house in a rural area, knowing there would be fewer fears and that my functioning would be better.

Dr. Manuel Ramos, my third psychiatrist, was by far my favorite. He was personable, considerate, and very supportive. We met weekly for a two hour session and discussed life in positive terms. My first two therapeutic experiences had taught me that talking about life's negative side only elicited anxiety—he agreed.

One day when discussing my first psychiatrist's psychodynamic approach, Manuel's Spanish passion began to rapidly flow. "John," he snapped, "I did psychoanalysis and psychodynamic therapy for thirty years and they just don't work." His passionately spoken words have not been forgotten by me.

Although he was sensitive to my feelings, he occasionally lectured me about my refusal to take OCD medication. After a short lecture he usually said, "I keep forgetting it's your OCD that prevents you from taking medication."

"Not so Manuel. Your medication causes serious side effects and isn't a cure," was my usual response. Then we talked informally again.

Before he retired Manuel taught me the importance of a helping hand for OCD patients. He occasionally acted as a facilitator—he called a local dentist and explained my illness and encouraged Beth to also be a facilitator. "You're never going to get back into life," he often said, "unless someone gives you a push." Manuel reinforced my belief that a friendly and helpful therapist would most benefit me. Our close therapeutic relationship lasted for a year, and my OCD improved slightly.

As the days pass I realize that past therapies were cognitively driven. Transference psychotherapy, contrarily, is emotionally driven. I've got neurotic problems, no doubt, and "here's my chance to weed my garden," as Grace has said. These transference feelings encourage me forward as does my mind which loves to think about the unknown. "What is there to lose?" I ask myself in a moment of worry. "Not much," I answer, still, however, knowing there's a lot of unfamiliar territory ahead.

CHAPTER 7

Will no one tell me what she sings?
Perhaps the plaintive numbers flow
For old, unhappy, far off things,
And battles long ago.... (Wordsworth)

Reading this poem provides a caveat: "there are many unhappy, far off things...." And there is a life beyond therapy which waits for me. To this end, quickly and successfully resolving transference feelings is my challenge. Therefore, I shall focus aggressively on my childhood. Higher levels of emotion will bring about faster healing: feeling is healing, isn't it?

Two hours before therapy my thoughts drift to and fro between my childhood, Mother, and Grace. I anxiously await going to therapy and seeing her.

Session 8/03

Grace enters the reception area in a different attire. Her usual, long, floating dress has been replaced with baggy, black–plaid slacks and a black blazer. She greets me with a Pavlovian smile; I rise, and off we go to her office.

Once there Grace smiles remotely and with obvious forethought says, "I'm very sorry but I didn't have time to read your journal last week." Time is what she has the most of, I suspect, she is a part–time resident with a light patient load.

"That's OK," I stoically reply masking rejection feelings. Not long thereafter, these feelings force me into a Hamlet like role where long standing problems with my mother and father are rotely presented....

Still, those rejection feelings can't be shaken. Eventually, they cause me to speak suavely, looking at her teasingly, "Grace, I've dated over one hundred women in my teenage years." She raises her hand and places it under her chin in a fist like style, perhaps, a sign encouraging me to go on. "You know, I had all the women I wanted in my teenage years." My run on impulse continues, "I started dating when I was nine years old."

"Sounds like an awful young age to start dating," she comments, her affect concealed.

"You grow up fast in the city," I reply with a cocky, teenage exuberance. "Of course," I go on, "I didn't really start, you know, serious dating until I was almost twelve." I cognitively realize the arbitrary and impulsive nature of these exaggerated tales, nevertheless, it hasn't dissuaded me from expressing them.

When I finish Grace asks, "Why don't you tell me about your date at twelve?" Abruptly, feelings of insecurity emerge because my mother forced me to go on this date with Beverly who cornered me on her porch, kissed me, and scared the....

"Not much to that date," brashly I declare. "She was just a nice girl who couldn't keep her hands off me." I glance at her and measure her reaction—her eyes have become sharp with interest. Grace instantly inquires about another girl I dated at eighteen. My words are carefully phrased to make her feel jealous and rejected like me. When I finish she cooly lounges back in her chair, her expression languid.

No more energy here, I decide. So after a long pause, I change direction and say as casually as my feelings will allow, "I'm an expert at distancing myself from people. I've done it all my life, and," my tone raised, firm, "eventually I'm going to tire of therapy and leave *you*," putting the extra tonal emphasis on the word "*you*." Her eyes look flat and free of qualification.

"We're doing good work together," she quickly counters after a moment of hesitation, "and we have developed a solid therapeutic relationship. Please don't distance yourself from me. Remember even when you become angry you must keep coming back." She beams me a nice smile and concludes by saying, "Remaining in therapy is vital to your healing process. Please promise me you'll keep coming back," her mouth twisting into another smile, her voice ringing with benevolence.

At this signal from her, I answer, "Sure will," nodding my head, feeling relieved that those rejection feelings have departed.

Toward the end of the session, Grace asserts, "You can say anything in here. I want you to feel absolutely free to express yourself in anyway."

"That's good," I answer to myself, musing about the implication.

Grace, unexpectedly, remembers that I will be traveling south this weekend to celebrate my Grandmother's 100th birthday. "I'm concerned about you," she says comfortingly, "and I want to give you my home phone number. Please call me if you need me this weekend or anytime." Her look compelling, her comment unexpected—How wonderful that she has such a caring attitude toward me!

"Thanks!" I say feeling like a very favored child. "It's good to know you're concerned with my well being." Next, we dialogue for several minutes about my mother and father. She stands smiling, letting me know the session is over.

Session 8/03 One hour psychotherapy

f **(Father)** "limited intellect". . . .aggressive. . .viewed patient as completely incompetent; Mother "it was the women in my life who did me in"; and transference to me. Continues to use exposure at home. Is going on trip tomorrow O: Clean shaven, Good eye contact, opens doors. TP **(Thought process)** Logical; TC **(Thought content)** Negative; SI **(Suicide ideation)** Negative; HI **(Homicidal ideation)** Negative for Psychosis; Mood "good;" Affect Full, congruent, anger, resentment; after a child–like pout. Cog: **(Cognitive)** remained very alert, good–excellent insight, judgment. A/P Beginning dynamic treatment methods with strong transference themes of abandonment; dependency; shame at own perceived incompetence. Plan: Continue open—ended exploration of early relationships, identifying themes. I gave patient my home phone # and directions to call from parents' house if in distress.

CHAPTER 8

The day after therapy Beth and I drive five hundred miles to Grandmother's 100th birthday party. She is in good health and lives with Mother and Father. Many activities that had been unthinkable a few weeks ago will confront me this weekend, for instance, shaking hands, eating in a restaurant, and using a bathroom that eleven other people are using. As we arrive for the party apprehensive feelings arise in me, because this is the first time I shall see my "real" mother since my emotional transference. My internal affect toward her has been changing: there has been a distancing of feelings and behaviors toward her, not dramatic distancing, just less involvement in her neurotic life: I am beginning to drift, apprehensively, toward concern for my feelings.

On our arrival we immediately go to Grandmother's bedroom and greet her. As we chat I glance toward her bureau and see a picture of Mother at thirty. The remarkable resemblance between her and Grace takes me back. Beth is surprised too at the stunning resemblance.

"No wonder! You're in such a deep emotional state with Grace!" Beth expressively says. "Grace's eyes, hair, and facial lines are a replica of your mother's."

"No doubt about it," I answer holding the picture close and examining it intently.

"Especially their hair, John," Beth comments. "Both have dark, shoulder–length, curled at the bottom hair."

"Beth," I say, drifting into yesteryear, "I can remember 'such love' at five years old. There I was lying in bed and curling my mother's hair around my finger...." Conclusively we have found a visual genesis for my emotional linkage to Grace. Later that day Beth and I select several pictures to show her.

My dearest moment of the weekend occurs when I gently hold Grandmother's hand and kiss her. She is most delighted because we haven't touched in eight years and comments on how well I'm doing. Other family members say nothing about my changed behaviors; it is remarkable the fortitude God gives me.

While driving home I recite a Dickinson poem for Beth which sums up my feelings about Grace and Mother: I felt a cleaving in my mind//As if my brain had split//I tried to match it, seam by seam//But could not make it fit. So with this schism settled into my psyche, I arrive home.

The following week Beth and I attend Opera Time at University College. What a lovely night we spend listening to "Songs of the Gaslight Era." I feel relaxed in a different way and if there is such a thing as emotional calmness brought on by music this is it. While associating emotional calmness with turbulent transference feelings might sound contradictory, mercurial describes their relationship. I can easily feel when listening to music and thinking about Grace, anger, love, and rejection, all within a few minutes. Then in just an instant, a calmness descends upon me as if all is well within and without.

Sunday on our walk, Beth and I discuss my need for a second psychiatrist who will assume the facilitating role that Grace has abandoned. Because of psychiatry's rule of one therapist—one patient, Grace must make this arrangement.

Two hours before therapy my thoughts drift to and fro between Grace, Mother, and my childhood. I anxiously await going to therapy and seeing Grace.

Session 8/10

By the time Grace and I are seated in her office, an odd emotional aura has surrounded me. I do not know if she attracts me or repels me but only that somewhere deep inside me there is an unbreakable emotional bond with her. Without forethought, but with a deep undertone of energy, I say in a shallow, fading voice, "I love you." These tender, compelling words alarm me. I sit there for a moment watching her not sure what is happening with my heartbeat slowing. She is silent. Then I hurriedly say, my voice stronger, and my words surer, "I don't really mean 'love' I mean 'like' you."

Leaning forward in her chair, Grace says softly and invitingly, "Do you mean just like?!"

My eyes turn from her gaze and my head droops, "No!...No!" I stammer and sputter. "I really mean love. I love you." I've become paralyzed by her control and feel desperate and helpless. There's a long silence.

Anxiously now, with my composure slightly improved, I summarize my journal writings, then I ask her to arrange immediately for a second psychiatrist. "That's a great idea!" she enthusiastically responds. "It would be very helpful to have another psychiatrist to consult with. What type of psychiatrist do you want?"

"I want a psychiatrist who will assume your previous role...." Expanding on this idea, I further suggest a single woman who will take an interest in my writing and make me confront my rejection and AIDS fear....

"How many sessions each month do you want to meet with me?" she inquires appearing subdued and distant. Her face has become unexpressive.

"We can meet five sessions each month, and I'll meet three or four times with the other psychiatrist."

"I must speak," she answers quickly, "with my advisor about another psychiatrist. I'll let you know." Her indecisive response frustrates my need for closure.

"I've a surprise for you," I excitedly tell her as the session moves on. "I learned a lot about the origin of our transference last weekend." After handing her my mother's photograph, I remark, "You won't believe this!"

She draws herself up, crosses her legs, and intently examines the picture. Her look is excited as she says, "There's a striking resemblance!" focusing her eyes back on me and shortly on the picture again. "How old was your mother in this picture?"

"About thirty," I answer. Grace still stares at the picture, then she places it on the desk and asks.

"Can I keep it?"

"Sure you can. I have plenty." We dialogue about my

mother for several minutes. Toward the session's end she mentions our relationship.

"Transference is about 'our' personal relationship and 'our' interactions." She hesitates before speaking in a soft, low tone. "At some point you'll hate me." Disturbing feelings surface at her use of the word "hate."

"Please don't make me hate you.... Please don't," I beg in a childlike fashion, feeling overwhelmed by thoughts of hating her. My head droops; I feel alone and helpless.

"Don't worry about it. I won't make you hate me, but you will." She quickly proceeds on with her transference agenda, leaving me vacillating between chagrin and paralyzation—in sort of a trance. "Our transference components," she declares, "are to be 'aggression' and 'sex.' Freud," she continues in an academic lecturing tone, "believed all psychological healing took place through 'sex' and 'aggression' exploration...." Like a child listening to his mother's important words, I remain silent. The session comes to an end with me in a pitiable state of discomposure.

No psychiatric record sent

Grace is on vacation for a week. Writing about family and childhood conflicts occupies my time. Eventually, however, to escape mounting latent feelings that are surfacing, I begin writing a detective story and love story.

Several hours before therapy my thoughts drift to and fro between Grace, my mother, and my childhood. I anxiously await going to therapy and seeing her. It has been a long ten days, and I miss her.

Session 8/21

Sitting in the reception area I feel emotionally tormented, and I wonder if finding the worst of my past is my healing price. I cannot believe, now, that all I wanted was OCD improvement.... Grace greets me with a warm smile. As we walk silently to her office, I mention my detective story; she ignores my comment.

Grace says after we are seated, "Being without me for a week must have been very upsetting for you?" Her expression is sympathetic, comforting. The feelings she wants from me are elicited: rejection, jealousy, and submission.

"Yes," I softly reply, feeling like a shy child again this session.

"Did you feel jealous and rejected because I left you and went away with Phil?"

"Yes, I did," I falter, my head turning from her look. I slowly begin recovering and begin to look at her as I say, "Well...No...I didn't miss you," those rejection feelings still stinging, "you all...that much." I defend, "And I'm going to distance myself from you.... I'm going to distance," she slightly leans back in her chair and smiles self–confidently obviously knowing it isn't true, "from you. I'm going to distance myself...." My words sound like the repeating of a mantra.

"Distancing is quite normal in a relationship like ours," counters Grace at my pause, "but promise me, no matter what," she insists vigorously and smiles, "that you will keep coming back. That's the important thing. You must," insisting again, folding her hands firmly together, "keep coming back! Promise me!" I nod in agreement.

"Therapy's about our love!" Grace says expressively with her eyes blazing in sincerity, "I want you to know this." My rejection feelings whimsically leave. After all, she has already told me how carefully she speaks, so her feelings must be strong enough to break through her circumspection.

"Wouldn't we be able to formulate a closer relationship if we met more often?" I suggest confidently after hearing her expressive words.

Her affect subtly changes, and she places her hand under her chin. Raw instinct and years of behavioral study tell me how much she likes my suggestion, although she says, "I have to think about it."

Later when I review last week's journal writings, Grace uncharacteristically takes copious notes. She aggressively interrupts my dialogue and repeatedly asks for restatements. After twenty minutes of her distractive note taking, I say,

"Your constant writing is disruptive. Could you stop? But, thanks for taking such an interest in me."

"Sure, I'll stop if it annoys you. Would you mind if I tape our sessions?"

"Certainly, you can tape them. That would be a lot better than note taking. Also," I go on, "I'll still be giving you my extensive journal writings where I describe our sessions."

"That's true, and I want you to keep writing that journal," she answers. Grace astonishes me when she casually remarks, "Sometimes I will spend three or four hours reviewing one of our sessions." She walks me to the door, stands close to me, and smiles as I leave. Tension buzzes in me because I know the love, sorrow, and anger of the past will come back if I can go beyond emotional bewilderment.

No psychiatric record sent

On the way home I tell Beth that therapy has become dynamic and contradictory. "Last week," I say, "Grace told me that I would hate her and that therapy should be oriented toward sex and aggression. This week she tells me therapy is about 'our love.'" Beth understands my concern; she is also confused about these things.

"Why," I repeat, "does she encourage me to love and hate her? to speak words of sex and aggression toward her? Grace has told me her job is to reformulate my mother image. But, what kind of mother image is she giving me?"

"John! Why don't you ask her to explain the relationship between love/hate and sex/aggression in more detail?" inquires Beth, mimicking my concern.

"Occasionally I've done that. But Grace responds by saying, 'Don't worry about these things, I know what I'm doing!'" My misguided logic turns to quizzical, "Anyway, questioning her is difficult because bringing up feelings is more compelling than discussing issues. Today is an example of that, she never explained anything in detail, and I just wanted to feel."

"Oh!" Beth replies with an instruction, "We better think and talk in more length about these concerns...."

Over the next several days we do exactly that, and eventually we conclude that if the past comes back to me the expression of latent aggression feelings will not come easily. I fear verbal aggression. In childhood, when I was verbally aggressive toward my parents, Father would verbally overpower me and Mother would insist that I was acting like Father and make me feel terribly insecure and rejected. If I became more verbally aggressive toward her, she would become cold and tell me she was becoming sick. Like the distraught soul in Munch's etching, *The Scream*, I want to scream in anger at the verbal aggression that disrupted my young life and the emotional confusion it caused me when searching for an adolescent identity. Much aggression toward my parents is buried in my subconscious, no doubt. If Grace forces me to hate her, an inappropriate and embarrassing transference dynamic may occur.

Yet, within the plains, and caves, and caverns of my memory there are also love feelings. Love was there in my childhood. The love I have for my parents is cloaked and needs to be found. How often I listened and empathized with Mother as she complained about the misery in her life, Father. My love was shown by focusing on her—her needs and her feelings. My love for her was internalized as "worry." In those instances when I felt for myself, guilt followed: I had been thinking of myself and not worrying, "loving" her.... But love is there!

Today, my mind ranged from one point of logic about my family and therapy problems to another, finally settling on a Shakespeare soliloquy:

> Why must I speak of it? Why must I always
> Stoop from this decent silence to this phase
> That makes a posture of my hurt? Why must I
> Say I suffer?....or write out these word....

Drifting thoughts and feelings between my own mother, whom I know quite well, to my surrogate mother, whom I barely know, to what's in my subconscious mind, which I don't know, describe what's happening this afternoon. Perhaps, I'm drifting away from my true self, and Grace is responsible. With this in mind, I write about Grace.

From our first session Grace presented herself differently than other professionals. The long, shapeless dresses she wore reminded me of my youthful 60's days, and she wore German–style house slippers made with heavy boiled wool. Even during warm summer sessions, she covered all parts of her body except for her hands and head; for instance, she might wear an unmatched blazer over her ankle–length dress. In every session she had an unkempt look. Her clothing was often wrinkled. She wore no makeup or jewelry, only a wedding band, and her beautiful dark hair was usually unbrushed. While Grace is not stunning, she is attractive. Her wonderfully projected smile, that came and went in just an instant, charmed me.

After four or five sessions it was obvious she was indecisive. At times she appeared nervous and self–absorbed, especially at the session's end. When I asked for appointment cards so I could touch aversion objects, she handed me one card with a wrong date, two with the wrong times, and she signed them variously as G. Tyre, Tyre, Grace, Tyre, G. etc. In one session she told me how carefully her words were thought out and commented, "I couldn't deal with saying the wrong thing to you."

CHAPTER 9

For the past several weeks, Beth and I have been dancing nightly in our living room. Last night was no different; we danced for three hours. I feel youthful when holding her and my touch elicits similar feelings from her. We hold hands and express intimate feelings more frequently—spontaneous youthful love–making has become familiar—our affects are changing. An emotional energy drives me even though I sleep only four hours a night.

Today, Beth and I walk hand in hand through our flower covered pasture. A warm sun, lucid blue sky, and Beth's touch bring forth feelings. I pick a bouquet of wild flowers and after returning home sit them on my desk and write the following:

I picked a bouquet of flowers in a field but did they care? One faintly whispers in my ear, "On the loam, in a vase, or in your hand, our purpose is to nurture earth's beauty until our time on earth is through." There are twelve flowers in my vase: six yellow, three lavender, two soft–white, and one reddish–orange. Oh, how their colors make me wonder if God does most like yellow, still, each displays a particular fairness.

A compelling yellow one catches my eye. It has five petals all distinct and two unopened buds ascend between each petal to make their presence known. Another yellow flower just appears, and it, too, has five petals and dainty black shoots caress its center. There is the alluring lavender flower which stands straight and tall on a frail pillar; I wonder how it stands so straight in nature's mighty wind, and it has such silky petals which form a little cup, perchance, to catch a tear.

Another flower, a lavender one, caresses my palm and is so slight. It has eight flowers on a thin stem with each having three petals, and its radiance lies in the sum. One flower looks quite confused. It has many yellow petals in a cluster, but a cluster with a gap; maybe, this flower leaves a gap to find more beauty? The red and orange flower is the brightest and has three buds; however, there are no leaves on its stem; perhaps, a sign from God that the world needs differences. Only one flower draws my thoughts to love. Its petals are clean, and white: cheery, and show much difference—a few are closed, yet some are open. The final one, I suspect, is not a flower but just a weed. It is prettier than the others and has petite, white petals tinged with black all bunched in a compelling array.

Grace loves flowers and this story may be written for her. I need her love, too. Feeling through subconscious wishes and desires is like holding a tiger by the tail: "I don't want to hang on but, also, I can't let go."

Cognitively, my feelings toward Grace are clearly: irrational, disturbing, and dominating. No matter how hard I try, they can't be explained away. Cognitive notions like "she's my surrogate mother" won't resolve them; they will have to work themselves out. Logic works against emotion like waves against the ocean. Believing this, I tap into feelings and begin thinking about Grace in romantic ways. It's not difficult because she has been constructed by my inner mind, with great cunning and startling intent, solely for the purpose of arousing emotion. Fortunately there are no undesirable consequences for expressing emotions in therapy.

Session 8/28

As we walk toward her office, Grace says seeming quite pleased, "I've spoken with Dr. Rudolph Miller, my advisor, and he has suggested we meet as often as you want. Freud," she continues, " believed a patient should meet every day with his or her therapist, even on weekends."

"Great," I reply once seated. My prediction that she wants more sessions with me proves accurate.

"I've also arranged for you to go to behavioral medicine."

"Why there?!" I interrupt in a challenging tone. Grace senses, quite correctly, that I'm annoyed because she hasn't arranged for another psychiatrist.

"Do you think," Grace counters sharply with a hard tone, "I would send you over there to be treated like a number?! Don't you think I am going to carefully arrange for your good care?! The trouble is that you don't have any trust in me!" Then she hesitates, flashes a splendid smile, and goes on to say, "I'm in an irritable mood today," hesitates again, smiles, " and I guess I'm looking for an argument."

"I'm already doing things to challenge my OCD. Why I've just walked through the hospital with you!" I retort, countering her reasoning again.

"Listen, you're unfamiliar with behavioral therapy; they can 'really' help you. That's why I'm sending you there!"

"Okay, I'll go," reluctantly I concede with a nod, feeling like my mother is making me go on another date.

"My therapeutic plan," she now tells me, "has been the same as yours, except, I didn't want to tell you. And your wonderful OCD improvement," she asserts, ignoring my belief that God has brought about my healing, "is due to 'spontaneous remission.'"

"Then, why is she sending me to behavioral medicine?" I ponder with confusion. Feelings of disappointment with her explanation about my OCD improvement unpredictably change; even if she is irritable, we are going on a romantic walk, I decide.

"If I've aggressive feelings toward you," I coyly ask, "can I express them?"

"Of course, you can say anything in here, anything."

"If I've romantic feelings toward you, can I express them?"

"Of course," she speedily reemphasizes, "you can say absolutely anything in here."

"I've romantic feelings toward you, and we're going on a special outing today."

Appearing captivated by my idea, she asks, "Where?"

"Here's the setting," I begin with a slight smile: "It's a beautiful day. The sun shines brightly but occasionally falters behind a scenic cloud. We are walking through the mountainous countryside and there's no one there but us. After catching the musty scent of a swamp, we start up the trail. The forest is brilliant with fall foliage. Amber, red, and yellow maple, birch, and beech leaves drop gently upon us as we amble along. A rough and rugged trail confronts us, and I watch your every step to make sure you are safe and secure. By noon we reach the place I've so carefully selected for our lunch, a lovely place on a cliff overlooking the glacier lake, but I am afraid, not because of the cliff's height, but because I desperately want you to like my special spot and fear that you will not.

Then as we sit and talk, I set out a special lunch I've prepared for you, a vegetarian lunch made only from flowers and wild edible plants. We eat orange nasturtiums, blue borages, and yellow calendulas in a salad of dandelion greens, followed by wild edible burdocks, palmetto roots, and Canadian thistles cooked in a secret sauce. To take the chill off, we sip rose hip tea. Everything has been prepared with only you in mind."

Grace seems charmed by my description and smiles occasionally. Our eyes have become yoked as I continue, "Then I place a blanket on the ground, and we lie on it, not side by side but end to end, with our heads gently touching. Our thoughts turn to each other's inner secret part as we glance toward the radiant heavens and talk." I pause and say, "My fantasy is over."

"Are you getting aroused thinking of me? Do you feel sexually excited by me now, sitting here?!" Grace shifting forward in her chair, fervently responds.

Startled, I reply, "No! I don't feel sexually aroused toward you," although I delight in her sexual innuendo that she has become aroused thinking of me. Still, Grace has misinterpreted my casual flirtation. "Grace, our casually romantic day doesn't have to end in sex. Does it?"

In a visibly self-conscious manner she fires several questions at me, "Would you take such a walk with another man? Would you let your wife do it with another man...?"

Breaking her off abruptly, I interrupt her censure, "Can't a man and woman," I persist, "have casual romantic feelings without being sexually aroused? Do they have to step over the threshold into sex?" The phone rings. She appears relieved. Her next patient is waiting. The session ends in disarray. A lot has happened this session, and my mind is fully confused.

Session 8/28 One hour psychotherapy No meds.

Discussed erotic transference to me and his difficulty relating to women. Continues with exposure work. After discussion with my supervisor, we will increase sessions to biweekly to increase transference and increase efficacy of dynamic treatment. Case discussed with supervisor Dr. Rudolph Miller both last week and today. Thought Process logical and coherent Thought content negative for suicidal ideation negative for homicidal ideation negative psychosis. Mood "good." Affect full, congruent. A/P Stable, engaged in psychotherapy without difficulty containing affect. Return to Clinic in 3 days. App't planned with Behavioral Medicine.

While driving home I say to Beth, "Expressing romantic feelings to Grace has only complicated therapy."

"Why?" asks Beth.

"She wanted to know if I was sexually aroused."

"Were you?" Beth responds with an apprehensive look.

"No!" quickly and empathically I answer, " the emotions I feel for her aren't like that. I'm interested in having her like me, even love me as strange as that seems, but not sexually!"

"It seems strange, but let's wait and see what happens," Beth encouragingly says, knowing that I'm improving and we are committed.

For the next several days my thinking and writing arbitrarily change. I write about Ruth first, next my family, and finally, Grace's sexual innuendo. Then I, driven by feelings, write about a sexual relationship that occurred thirty years ago.

Jane, my partner, was a delightful person, and we had

pleasurable sex together.... Remembering back to the way I had been, fiery, spontaneous, and passionate, evokes youthful feelings and exaggerated writings which create more youthful feelings, an addictive process if there ever was one....

That evening Beth reads my writings. When she finishes I quickly speak, "It's hard to understand what's happening. Jane just popped into my mind and I wrote about her. And when I wrote about Grace's romantic walk, I thought about Ruth and you more than her."

"You never told me about your relationship with Jane," Beth remarks with a hint of jealousy in her voice.

"Well, it wasn't that much," I answer wondering if I hadn't mentioned Jane casually over the past twenty–six years. "Beth," I go on, carefully forming my words, "writing about past experiences releases intense, irrepressible, perplexing feelings; nevertheless, they decrease my anxiety. It's addictive...."

We talk for several hours about therapy's romantic orientation and how my feelings may be released. I'm in a whimsical emotional state although I try to be sensitive to Beth's feelings.

"You've been changing," Beth says, noticing my youthful affect. Nevertheless, a tinge of uncertainty surrounds her encouragement. It's true what Beth has said, that I'm becoming emotionally altered, but it's alteration mostly through youthful impulse.

"Grace tells me that my feelings should be directed at her. And that therapy's all about sex and aggression, so maybe...." My words just drift away because we know what has been implied. "Better to do it than describe it to Beth," good sense tells me.

Sorting through "things" is becoming more difficult for my cognitively oriented mind: logic is being replaced with emotion. Emotion tells me to think of therapy as a construct, play, or movie, not real life. The result: I'm thinking less about consequences. On the other side a perturbing question arises in my cognitively oriented mind, perhaps, all these emotions are meant to lie there restlessly and without "resolution." And so, with this schism of go and stop lodged in my mind, the search for sexual feelings toward Grace begins anyway.... That long forgotten part of me, the carefree self, I most want to remember, has emerged.

Session 8/31

Immediately after entering her office, Grace apologizes with a bashful smile, "I'm sorry that I asked if you were getting aroused thinking of me last session. Please continue," she softly murmurs, "with your fantasy. I want to hear more."

"Don't you remember it was finished last session?" She puts her hand under her chin and stares at me like she hasn't remembered. Her dark eyes tease me forward.

"Don't worry, I have another one this week," I confidently reply. But first here's a printout of Webster's definition of romantic. "See," I wait as she reads it, "Webster's definition of romance supports me."

"Forget about semantics!" she snaps, clearly showing me that her intellectual authority doesn't like a challenge. "I don't want to deal with you in these kinds of ways. Therapy's about expressing feelings not debating definitions!"

"OK!" I reply. "Grace, I'd like to take you dining and dancing at an intimate spot. Let's explore those erotic feelings you're after," smiling at a pause, "Do you like wine?" She looks at me blankly. "Do you," repeating again, "like wine?"

"Let's," she insists adjusting her seat slightly, "return to last session's fantasy with me."

"No, I'm not going back there with you." My response is cold, rejecting; nevertheless, it is tempered with a fine male smile. Her comment and failure to answer my question has annoyed me. She's running toward feelings and we both know it. Transference emotions are flowing as I continue.

"Why don't you tell me how much you like me?" Grace remains silent. "Don't you like me," I say holding up my two fingers and closing them together, "just a tiny–little–bit?" She places her hand under her chin and stares, her look becoming unsettled. She's feeling a lot, I sense.

"You can't be acting a role like this!" she asserts adjusting her dress. "What's happened to you?! Can you explain why you are so different today?!"

"Nothing's different," I respond suavely. "I'm showing you the more romantic side of my nature," another attractive smile from me. "Do you like it?" I say softly, letting my voice drift off.

In a nervous manner she finally says expressively and boldly, "I can't get involved with you! Adding after a long hesitation, "I'm a professional therapist!" Then, perhaps, in a softer tone of disappointment, she repeats, "I can't get involved with you, I'm a resident therapist." Her innuendo that "that's" my only barrier is crystal clear. Then quickly she says, "I have to expect this from you. You're an experienced therapy patient."

"Not like this," I wryly think. The phone rings and she talks for a couple of minutes to another psychiatrist. By the time she hangs up my transference feelings have settled down. Grace appears tired so I apologize for my intensity. She emphasizes that I'm doing the right thing.

"I was on call last night," she says seeming self–absorbed. Then she adds, "Some sleep is what I need to get myself straightened out."

"How about," I request, boyishly, on my way out, "giving me a big smile." Her brilliant smile is the last thing I see as I head down the hallway. The smile makes me feel like an adolescent swaggering home from a fun date.

Session 8/31 One hour psychotherapy
S/O Continued to discuss erotic transference and his need to control relationships with women. Continues with exposure work, continues writing and functioning well. Affect slightly constricted, tense. Mood 'good;' negative suicidal ideation; negative homicidal ideation; negative for psychosis. A/P Stable and engaged in therapy. Return to Clinic in 4 days.

Today, a vortex of anxiety surrounds me. To extricate

myself from it, I obsessively write. Explaining feeling driven behaviors is like calculating the never ending square root of "pi." My calculations for therapy behaviors go like this: justification, it's transference therapy; blame, it's my lousy childhood that must be worked through; and sexual encouragement, Grace entices these behaviors from me.

In a uniquely different way, I think quietly as I head to therapy: "When all the subterfuge is done//I choose, me: talk romance and find that me."

Session 9/07

Grace is pleasant, but distant, as the session opens. She sits further from me and uncommonly leans back. Her nonverbal messages are getting easier and easier to read. While I won't say too much here about this, I occasionally taught nonverbal communication.

Her distant look brings out rejection feelings although, I suspect, she's only hiding from her feelings. I hand her last week's journal and discuss its content. Romantic feelings and my need for her love pull me along. So, then, smiling, leaning slightly forward, I begin, "I've decided on another trip for us this week. It will be a fun place to go." She holds her distant posture as I say, "We're taking this week's journey to Northern Thailand where I'll introduce you to some charming people." Recollecting this experience elicits sentimental feelings. "The Black Hills people," I go on, touching the escarpment of the past, "have a kind and gentle nature with uniquely sincere smiles...," I drift through thoughts about playing with the children and helping them fish, there are flowing thoughts about their food, dress, and culture.... Caught in the mood, memory after memory appears, feeling after feeling arises....

At a pause Grace interrupts, "Would you take me out in Bayview where I live?" Her words startle me.

"Well! Of course! I'd take you out anywhere." I stop to gather my thoughts, but her suggestion has elicited strong feelings so I go on, "I still have these powerful transference feelings for you." She has leaned considerably forward in her chair now but doesn't respond. For several minutes, I describe my transference feelings. From time to time she adjusts her seat position, but Grace never takes her eyes from mine.

In a whimsical way perhaps to build a subliminal tension, I deliberately lull for several seconds, then say, slowly, forming my words carefully, "I want you to know I see you beyond the real, beyond the now, and beyond the here." She slides her chair forward, putting her hand under her chin. Our eyes are only six inches apart and have melted together. Her warm breath is pouring over me. I delay to enjoy this intimate moment and summon up my courage to say, "Do you understand what all this means?" She nods once, then twice very slowly, but doesn't speak a word because she is enmeshed in her world like I in mine. Her warm breath is still pouring over me.

There's a long silence where we savor the result of our weakness. Finally, Grace moves her chair back and speaks, "What kind of role do you want me to play?"

I look at her, confused, "Didn't we go over that quite a few sessions ago?"

"Tell me again," she softly requests.

"You know, a friendly, concerned therapist who will help me when needed...."

"By the way," I say, my tone tender, "do you know you're hurting my feelings?"

"How?"

"You've been dressing–up for your advisor the last two weeks. Why don't you dress–up for me next session." Her response is nothing graphic. For the remainder of the session, I glide through feelings and speak unrelated words. Grace offers up a smile as I leave the office. As I walk down the hallway two questions swirl in my brain like debris in a tornado: "What's happening? Where are we heading?"

Session 9/7 One hour psychotherapy

Patient continued to discuss erotic transference; was able to offer some criticism of my therapeutic approach, express rejection and anger appropriately. Continues playing tennis, interacting socially. Affect: Full, congruent; negative suicidal ideation; negative homicidal ideation; negative for psychosis. A/P Stable engaged continue dynamic therapy.

Beth is troubled when I arrive in the lobby. Earlier Grace ignored her as they passed in the hallway as Beth began speaking to her.

"She might not have seen you."

"John, you're not.... It's not so," counters Beth shaking her head expressively. "I don't understand why she's been rude—looking right at me and then turning her head deliberately away as we passed."

"Let's get coffee and play tennis," I answer, refusing to recognize the implication.

"OK," Beth replies, sensing I have had enough therapy for today.

Over the next several days my cognitive mind is called upon to "sort through a maelstrom of emotion." Nothing, however, is accomplished as emotion drives my thinking to and fro. One emotion is constant, however, the love I hold for Beth which I won't destroy for anything.

Adolescent feelings of turmoil and confusion spiral around the camouflaged anger toward my parents as I write. The positive is ignored. Instead, the focus is on two troubling teenage relationships. As therapy time approaches, I am disappointed with Grace because she hasn't called me by name or arranged that behavioral medicine appointment.

My thinking heading for therapy—don't expose anymore love feelings because you'll only get hurt through disaster. The rejection and sorrow of the past have come back to haunt me.

Session 9/11

Today, she not only greets me without her customary smile, but she has dressed up for me as requested: makeup, hair styled, dangling hoop earrings.... An ill–gotten rush of ecstasy flows within me. She has made me remember the way

I had been: sensual and angry at an old girlfriend for her rejection.

Once seated, I devote several minutes telling Grace about my fear of being verbally aggressive toward women. "My mother," I say, my tone raised, "dealt with my criticism and aggression by being sick and going to bed. Even a minor criticism could send her to bed for a week or two." Grace leans back in her chair with her hands together as I continue, "When Mother was sick I felt it had been my fault and that I had had some majestical power over her.... It was a scary power for a child to face. Eventually, I avoided any criticism toward Mother for fear of making her ill.... I guess at some point I began thinking of women as defenseless and frail...." From one point of emotion to another I go—rejection to denial, distress to consternation, and then the short journey to rebellion.

Grace is not responding, her dark eyes distant, so I snap, "The same thing's true in here! You can't take any criticism either!" She replies with a cold, glaring stare. "Take my name," I'm now speaking slowly and carefully, allowing reason to hold back anger, "I've been in therapy with you almost four months and you've only called me by name once, and only at my direction. You agreed months ago to call me by name but haven't done it. Why? My previous psychiatrists all called me by name.... Why won't you do it?"

Sitting almost like a statue in a chair, she remains silent, and I feel deflated like a limp balloon but continue anyway, "Calling people by name is important. Haven't you ever heard someone say, I hate being treated like a number?" I lull and watch. Her look tells me she's not going to reply. After a few more examples which do no good, I raise my appeal, "Have you ever read Alexander Solzhenitsyn's book, *The Gulag Archipelago*?" Grace remains silent. "It's a story of dehumanization and one technique is to make people nameless. How about," I realize, however, my circumstance is trivial in comparison, "name dehumanization with war prisoners and Holocaust victims." By now, I feel like a child begging over and over again for recognition. Why, for such an easily resolved issue, does she make me go to this extreme? If there is therapeutic evidence for not calling me a name, then why doesn't she present it?

"More and more," forcefully I state, "your behaviors are becoming chaotic. Just look at what's happening today. You won't say a word, you won't respond. You're only staring, never even blinking. Stability in my therapist is important."

Once again she doesn't respond, and I feel like she's trying to frustrate me. Finally as the session ends, I mention no one has contacted me from behavioral medicine. "I'll consider your requests and look into your appointment," she answers looking at her clock, quickly saying, "Your time's up for today."

Walking toward the hospital lobby, I'm telling myself, "My points are valid and should be considered from the doctor–patient level, but the reality is the transference bond can't be broken, and she knows it!"

Session 9/11 One hour psychotherapy
Continues to explore aggression; describes strong feelings of anger, and a sense of being rejected by me. Has not heard from behavioral medicine despite my consult weeks ago; I had spoken with them circa ten days ago and heard they were attempting to contact patient with a female therapist. Continues to play tennis, but is expressing concern and anger regarding not having behavioral medicine. Negative suicidal ideation; negative homicidal ideation negative psychosis. A/P stable, but I share patient's concern that we have behavioral med follow–up to maintain stability. Engaged in therapy but with some increased resistance. Will discuss with Dr. Miller. Will contact behav. medicine today.

Therapy is discussed on our drive home. With a discouraged tone I comment to Beth, "Therapy's more and more confusing. Grace seems to be rejecting me through silence and disinterest."

"Listen," replies Beth, "take each session as it comes.

You're getting a chance to sort through your adolescent and childhood feelings, and it would be foolish to resist."

"Well...Well," I answer with a slight shrug of my shoulders. "I guess you're right. Nevertheless," I continue in an emphatic tone, "here's a prediction, call it the Nostradamus syndrome: next week she will agree to using my name again but never will! She's just like my mother, her pleasure and power come from not doing what she's agreed to do." The gravel of the driveway tells us we are home.

My writings this week are mostly about my mother and chaotic therapy. In preparation for the next session, I decide to look into Grace's eyes, find my mother, and bring out childhood feelings. Transference is like an emotional torture chamber of distortion and magnification, although, perhaps, contrary to the real thing, positive changes may come from it. Feeling is the road to healing, so I've been told.

CHAPTER 10

This session I have a plan to exorcise suppressed emotions.

Session 9/14

Grace is personable as the session begins, and I'm nervous as usual. "I've decided to call you by name," she opens and pauses to watch my reaction which is nothing descriptive; she proceeds, "How do you want to be addressed?"

"It really doesn't matter," I reply, smiling, coalescing, not wanting to annoy her.

"Well, I'll call you Mr...."

"Call me Doctor! I've worked hard for that title," I interrupt in a firm tone. "I'd like that—Doctor Tyre!" Her veiled attempt to reject me is annoying.

"We'll...OK," Grace agrees giving a slight nod as I wryly speculate—she'll never say my name, anyway. The subject changes and we discuss my journal for sometime.

Shortly it changes again when I say, "Grace, do you remember your behavioral medicine referral? They've never contacted me." She leans back in her chair, her face stern and set like my mother's under criticism.

"I'm very busy," she coolly remarks, hesitates and, then, abruptly counters with eyes fixed on me, "You know, I'm only in my office one and one–half days a week, but I'll check with them when I have time."

"It is ludicrous and troubling," I tell myself, "that she has been too busy for weeks to walk next door, pick up a phone, or have her secretary call. Time is not the real issue, there must be something else? In most sessions she has kept me beyond our time, and Joan, her secretary, has told me she has few patients."

As the session unfolds Grace begins to stare and refuses to dialogue. So I stop talking and look straight ahead into her eyes. The office is distressingly quiet as I search to find my childhood mother in her. Feelings surface quickly, and I respond, "I hate you and I will pray for your death."A powerful surge of latent anger has surfaced. "What do you think of that? How does it make you feel?" I say. Grace remains silent; her posture is still. "I hate you and I will pray for your death." Another surge of latent anger surfaces. Grace interrupts this chantlike soliloquy and tries to direct my expressions toward my family. "Why are you trying to deflect the anger," I rebukingly reply, my tone quivering, "away from yourself?! You're just like my mother; you look and act like her.... Nobody was better at deflecting my anger and not empathizing with me than she was! She always let others make her decisions so she could blame them! Deja vu in here...." By now, the emotion has dissolved, leaving me spent and weak, but clearheaded. Expressing these feelings has been cathartic. Grace looks at me intently, hopefully, she senses that I hate no one and I'm only reliving a childhood nightmare.

"No matter how hard you pray for my death," she says intently, "I'm not going to die for you. So you can keep praying but nothing is going to happen to me!" By the time my mind clears of thinking only about myself and not the ultimate, that is—sowing more and more seeds whose only crop would be grief—Grace has ended the session and risen from her chair. As I take my first step toward the door, she comments in a soft and caring voice, "I want to tell you that patients who have disclosures like this may mutilate themselves. For instance, they start cutting their arms and face." She hesitates to measure my reaction. I am functioning with disquieting resilience. Some never atrophying instinct has warned me to show her no alarm. "But don't worry," she smoothly continues leading me to the door, "it just happens with some people." Her tranquil words are unrepresentative of what she's implying, and I sense she has an ulterior motive far beyond a desire to help me. If so, we have entered into a relationship that goes beyond that of patient and therapist. Why has she waited until the end of the session to suggest such an alarming possibility? Doesn't she understand the

OCD mind? I'll obsess about her comment for....

Session 9/14 One hour psychotherapy (Wrong date—This session should be 9/25)

Patient discussed and demonstrated extensive angry transference, but without any inappropriate acting out. Continues to play tennis and be active outside the house. Denies suicidal ideation/psychotic symptoms. ETOH 1–2 beers on some evenings. Continues to journal extensively. Stable, engaged in transference. Return to clinic in 4 days.

"Grace," alarmingly I say to Beth in the lobby, "has told me I might begin mutilating myself with a knife."

"Tell me exactly what she's told you," Beth calmly and authoritatively instructs.

"She said that people who make disclosures like praying for their parents death as a child may hurt themselves," I falter feeling distress and confusion. "That's everything she said."

"What kind of psychological symptoms occur before it happens?"

"She didn't say."

"What did she tell you to do? Me to do? And what's she going to do if....?" Not wanting to alarm me further, Beth redirects my thinking by saying, "John you don't have a history of this, so we shouldn't worry."

"You're right Beth. But why is she inserting this horrible thought into my mind? It's the twilight zone with her," I sardonically reply. "Beth, maybe I shouldn't be thinking of my childhood and keeping a journal. It's too disruptive...." My mind sputters to a stop like a stalling car engine; then, I say after a long pause, "Let's get a cup of coffee and play tennis."

"Sounds good," replies Beth; nonetheless, her face shows an unspoken concern. "Did she agree to call you by name?"

"She agreed to, but guess what? She didn't!" Our smiles in harmony become a tension reliever.

Obsessive minds, I know, can't always resolve fear ideation; I think as we head toward the tennis courts, hopefully, I can control it, be able to turn it off, but fear ideation scares me like red sky in a sailor's morn.

CHAPTER 11

I have found a powerful propensity to bring forth childhood transference feelings. It has become easy to feel what I want and to willfully decrease those feelings. How deep must I delve? I am diligently ripping apart my emotional foundation, but where is the therapeutic structure to create a new one? When the winter frost comes it will be too late for rebuilding....?

Last week I journalized about two unresolved adolescent behaviors. Today as I approach the reception area, they seem very important, although by today's social standards they aren't much. Still, these conflicts lay deep within my early Christian training. The cathartic effect of telling Grace, hopefully, will release the guilt. Even Beth doesn't know about them.

Session 9/18

Once seated Grace manufactures a smile and the session begins. "Have you read the detective and love story chapters I gave you last week?"

"I loved your detective, Lt. Schwein. He's a most interesting and delightful character," Grace replies with a broad smile.

"There's a lot of me in him," I respond with a wink, delighted by her sparkling review.

"Do you think I should finish the story and try to sell it?"

"I'd buy it!" encouragingly she replies.

"How about my love story?"

"Well...Well," she hesitates, simpers and coyly says, "I think we should talk about Bettina some other time."

"But why? Didn't you like 'Bettina' the main character? She's quite a woman," provocatively I reply, allowing my words to drift off....

Grace leans forward in her chair, smiles again, and after taking a light breath she says, "We're going to talk about this later." Casual flirtations are becoming commonplace and a tension reliever.

The session continues to unfold as I say, "I'd like to tell you about two troubling, adolescent reminiscences, one at thirteen and the other at fourteen." Grace rocks back in her chair and postures herself with a stare. "It's difficult for me to tell you about them." Finally yielding to guilt's finger of blame, I begin. Grace maintains her silent posture as each memory is confessed. I tell her about them in a hushed church tone.... Agony and shame increase as I speak; the ache of my conscience has become sharper.... There's a time when I become silent for a minute, the experience of this one memory has become so fresh and painful I can't form a thought, much less words to describe it..., my voice barely above a whisper. The words hurt.... I smile weakly and shrug when finished. For a moment, I silently linger in the troubled sorrow from the past. Then I say "Well...!" She doesn't respond. "I guess.... Well...," pausing once, feeling confused and, then, rotely saying, "Don't you know I'm finished?"

"Why are you telling me these things?!" she asserts, coldly and rejectingly.

"Well...I, just.., ah..., well...," I swallow hard, my mind racing through my options as I try to come up with some excuse. Quickly I answer, "I thought talking about sex was the last thing to do before I left therapy.... You know...." Feeling lost, my words taper off. There's an eon of silent staring between us. Presently I return to criticizing the chaos and confusion in therapy that has once again left me "hanging" by a thread.

"How can I," feeling as rejected as a child not invited to a friend's party, "trust you as my doctor. You display less and less interest in me as a patient. You've agreed to call me by name and you're still refusing to do so! How about my behavioral medicine appointment.... You're acting more and more chaotic: smiling, staring, frowning. I never know what to expect or do...," and so, on and on it goes. I ramble and Grace stares, never blinking or moving in her seat....

"How does it feel to have such a lousy therapist?" she

finally speaks, perhaps, to make me feel guilt and evoke empathy feelings toward her.

Catching me in her undertow, I answer, "You're really helping me," now only able to think of sheerly nervous and pleasant remarks.

"You're right," Grace joins in. "We are doing wonderful work together and have a solid relationship. Your therapy is going according to my plan." Grace then remarks in an energetic tone, "I want to assure you I'm a professional and things are going fine!"

Grace's amiable manner encourages me to ask about emergency support. While I am able to negotiate daily life under stable circumstances, a destabilizing situation, such as Beth being ill or needing emergency surgery may be different. "I'll be there for you, be it day or night," Grace says. "I'll just have to come out and respond to you differently," assuredly, decisively. "Your time's up," she finishes.

"Can I count on it?" I ask walking to the door.

Her final word is: "Absolutely!" I leave.

Session 9/18 One hour psychotherapy

Again explored aggressive transference to me; was able to eventually see this as transference, based on his relationship with his mother who he saw as inconstant and untrustworthy. Able to tolerate some expression of longing and grief as well as rage. Continues to be active and functional. Appt. scheduled with Behav Med for next Wednesday (Behav Med says they've tried repeatedly to call with this; patient states he is usually at home). A/P Continues engaged, working hard on key issues of rage, betrayal, trust. No meds, stable, Return to clinic 3 days.

When Beth and I arrive home, we relax by walking in the countryside. It troubles me to withhold these sex secrets from her so I tell her. Beth is sensitive and helpful with her probing questions and comments and healing takes place.

It has been a confusing and restless day and as bedtime approaches—eerily unsettled feelings surround me. At 12 A.M. I suddenly awake with an almost vivid childhood memory.

"God please open my mind further," I pray. A few minutes later there are feelings of intense fear as I think of Fluffy my cat. Sobs come quickly. Beth awakens, sits alarmingly up in bed, and asks, "Is everything OK...? Is everything OK, John?!!" There is no response from me because I'm shadowed by an indistinguishable fright, the fright from a sudden and unexpected clutch out of my mind's darkness. Almost imperceptibly an image clarifies. I'm fearing for my young life and lay in bed thinking of how I can kill my mother and father. My parents have killed my best friend, Fluffy, and I now believe they are going to kill me!

"I hate you both! I hate you both, and I'm going to kill you first!" Beth hears me scream in fearful rage.

"What's wrong?" Beth emphatically asks again with alarm. "Please, tell me John!" By now my composure has returned, although the desire to linger in the feelings and thoughts remain. "John," she says again, "what's wrong?!"

"Something very different...something scary," I slowly begin. "I have remembered the time my parents killed my cat."

"You mean Fluffy?"

"Yes," I quaver. "Every night as a six year old child my father let Fluffy lay with me until I fell asleep. I loved Fluffy and her companionship. One day I came home from school and found Fluffy missing, gone forever as it turned out. Mother told me they had given her to a farmer but she lied because she wouldn't take me to see her. I fought, I screamed, I begged her to bring my friend back, but she wouldn't."

"What a horrible thing to do to a child," Beth sorrowfully comments holding me and holding back her own tears.

"I really loved my cat," tearfully I reflect, glad for her touch. "You know Beth that my childhood home was violent, loud arguments, and the worst fights were at night. I had carried on all afternoon about Fluffy. That night the screams coming from their bedroom were worse. They had just killed my cat, and I feared that I would be next. I have always wondered why I was fearful of sleeping alone; perhaps, this is why!"

"Let's have a cup of tea," suggests Beth. We walk to the kitchen where a cup of tea settles my twitching nerves.

Later that night Beth is inquisitive and asks, "What does it feel like when you're going through a memory like this?"

"It's a strange thing," hesitating to gather my thoughts and, then, remarking, "I've never experienced anything like it in my life. I knew who I was, who you were and that you were beside me in bed, but I was lost in a rush of emotional childhood memory. There was no desire for me to answer you because I was afraid words might quickly alter feelings."

In bed again, my body feels emotionally drained, and I say, "You know Beth, my parents would absolutely never have physically abused me."

Beth quietly listens sitting nervously on the bed as I finish. Eventually she remarks, "I guess transference works this way. You experience latent childhood emotions from repressed memories, and, hopefully, by sorting through these feelings and memories your adult cognitive and affective structure can resolve them."

"I sure hope you're right—I sure hope so." My final words before drifting into a dreamless sleep.

Session 9/21

The receptionist tells me that Dr. Tyre will be delayed for awhile. Twenty minutes later an agitated, bearded man strides aggressively through the office doorway and walks hurriedly past Beth and me. Beth comments, "That psychiatrist is really angry."

"Maybe he and Grace were having a disagreement."

"What makes you think that?" inquires Beth.

"Grace told me her advisor had the 'neatest' beard and that he looked like Freud. That guy resembles Freud. Don't you think so?"

"He does somewhat," replies Beth. "I've seen him come out and greet patients and...." Before Beth can finish, Grace hurriedly approaches. Her hair looks like she's been running her hands through it. She seems emotionally upset and self–absorbed; her tenseness is contagious.

"I'm sorry to be late," she says once we are seated in her office.

"That's OK," I reply knowing that I need her today. Then I say, "I'm not anxious to explain what happened to me the other night, anyway."

"Tell me," directs Grace, absently, her eyes drifting to her desk clock.

A current of emotion rushes through me, profound and inescapable. My therapist seems to be in a sort of a trance as I enter the bad dream of my childhood. First, I pause for several seconds lost to myself in the memory of Fluffy; then I say, "The other night I frightfully remembered when my parents killed my cat." I waver and search for an emotional coupling. But not by the flicker of a brow or the movement of the smallest muscle does she give me attachment. Still anew, this nightmare, within a nightmare, draws me forward and is presented—an agonizing moment of emotional rebirth.... "That's how my parents took Fluffy...." The phone rings interrupting my final words. Grace talks for a minute and hangs up.

"What good," my voice low, shaky, "are these horrible memories?" I hesitate full of tired futility before continuing with a troubled thought, "I will just exchange neurosis A for neurosis B...," now hopelessly confused and desperate for an appropriate conclusion.... Silently I wait for a connection.

Finally, after several long minutes of silence between us, Grace speaks with no particular expression of interest, "How do you feel about what your parents did to your dog?"

Without a thought I vulgarly reply, "I felt like I'd been f—."

Grace notices my startled look and quickly responds, "So you felt like you'd been f—," her way of letting me know she doesn't mind saying f—.

"By the way Fluffy was a cat not a dog."

"Sorry," apologizes Grace looking at her desk clock, "it was a cat. That's right? We're almost out of time, so I want to tell you that your criticism of therapy," she forces a smile, "and your criticism of me are defense mechanisms."

I shrug and shake my head having no clue what the proper response is. Her statement like so many others has left me perplexed and frustrated. Then, instinctively, I answer with a rambling soliloquy, "But what am I defending against? I have written and spoken endlessly about my family relationships and the traumas of my life...." She stares, always silent. My mind leaking into wasteful self–conflict.... I persist, "In here my Achilles heel has been exposed. Is trying to get well, to do everything right to get well, a defense mechanism?!" There's a long silence where I think, "She seems so sane, so perfectly impregnable in her staring silence, but am I right?"

"Like I said, attacking therapy is a defense mechanism," and with a raised brow she stands and terminates our session.

Session 9/21 One hour psychotherapy. No medications
Patient explored traumatic childhood memory of parent's removing his dog **(Cat)** without telling him, either before or after; he assumed his dog, **(Cat)** was dead and in fact 45 years later his mother has admitted this. He felt as a five year old that his parents, especially his father, would kill him next, at night during one of their explosive arguments and recalls lying in bed listening to them argue, consumed with grief over his dog **(Cat)**, terror for his own life, rage at his parents. Was able to discuss how this loss led to a 'split' inside himself between the 'loving boy' and the romantic man, without communication between the two. **(Never discussed)**

Stable, with stable and minimal OCD symptoms, negative suicidal ideation, negative homicidal ideation, negative psychosis. A/P Is tolerating increasing affect. May be starting the process of recognizing his splitting of himself, and the world. Continue psychotherapy. Return to clinic 4 days.

On the long drive home, Beth and I disuss Grace's inattentiveness which has brought out rejection feelings in me. "It must have been difficult to be psychologically and emotionally by yourself when you described this traumatic incident!" empathetically, Beth remarks.

"You bet it was. Today, I traveled through therapy alone."

Beth encourages me not to de–energize myself by worry and remarks, "You're getting better although it's difficult for us."

"You're absolutely right. There's improvement, but Grace has commented that my therapy concerns are only a defense mechanism."

"What!" a surprised Beth replies. "How did she conclude that?"

"Who knows," I answer, shrugging my shoulders to let Beth know I've discussed enough therapy. Beth suggests that we head home and go for a long, long walk; I agree with her. Physical exertion tempers therapy's negative energy.

Session 9/25

Grace is tardy again this week. Upon her arrival she acts rejecting, not speaking, and distant, not smiling, toward me. In her office I plaintively ask, "Why are you keeping me waiting?"

She takes so long to answer, I'm not sure if she has heard me. "It' a time rejection," she finally says.

"Why are you trying to reject me, anyway? Is this how you're going to give me a new mother image by rejecting me like my mother did?"

A nervous undertone appears in her at this challenge. She starts rubbing her chin and recrosses her legs once, then again, and snaps, "We professionals know what we're doing. Let's move on!" Not only is she flexing her authoritative power, she has begun to savor it.

"Move on to where?" I think, momentarily drained of energy from her debasement.

An adversarial therapeutic tone, by her action, exists, so I say to mediate it, "Grace, don't you recognize the chaotic relationship we're creating...?" I hesitate, waiting for a response. But she refuses to speak. Her silence reflects her authority and my frustration, so I just proceed and remark, "This chaos is becoming emotionally addictive. It's bringing out feelings in us but so what? Where are we heading? that's the important question." I hesitate to gather my thoughts and listen for her reply, but she still remains wordless. A screaming silence is everywhere around us as I swallow hard and allow my mind to race through options.

We stare at each other for a minute, perhaps two. I realize I'm getting nowhere staring back at her, so I go on to say, "Our minds are interlocked at the subconscious level.... Can't you feel it! We've intertwined our emotional selves!" My precocious emotional temperament can no longer stand her neglect, so I snap, "How long is it going to be before I go stark, 'staring' mad in this room with you...! There's something wrong with this kind of therapy. Things are becoming too chaotic! Look now, you're glaring, gazing, and gawking at me...!" I'm absorbing her therapeutic madness as another shadow of discontent crosses my face. "Why are you trying to make me angry? Why won't you say anything?" Eventually, I pause exhausted, drained of thought. Enough has been said; after all, my words are being ignored. I sit with her in silence for fifteen minutes—wanting to be anywhere else in the world but in this crazy room.

When I can't take anymore silence, I speak lowering my voice and choosing my words carefully, "I'm starting to lose sight of you as a person and that's not good.... We need to foster a positive therapeutic relationship...." Her silent stare rejects my concern, so I suggest with harsh, angry words, "You're becoming my psychological whore!" She leans forward in her chair and unshutters that stare telling me she's ready to speak. At this sign I quickly snap again with a clear, firm tone, "You're just becoming my psychological whore, and I don't like it! It's not right!"

"That's what I'm here for," she says to my surprise. She pauses appearing lost in her inner self; then she asks, "Did you feel both love and rage when you were telling me these things today?"

"Of course not," I answer quickly, emphatically. "How can anyone feel love and rage at the same time?" This seems like a question designed to avoid and negate my therapeutic concerns. The room is again eerily quiet as she becomes silent, and I sense her aggression like a gazelle being stalked by a lioness. We stare at each other in silence for five, maybe ten minutes. As I turn away the phone rings ending the session. I quietly leave her office feeling the dull ache of her authority and manipulation. Why is she doing this to me? I wonder walking down the hall, and why have I let her? I have to put my mind somewhere else and get it off what she's doing. Use that thought as your emotional argument, I tell myself.

Session 9/25 One hour psychotherapy

Discussed anger at me and at his mother and grandmother; wondered if anxiolytics would help him at times when he is exhausted and agitated. Continues stable without suicidal ideation, homicidal ideation or psychosis; doing home exposure therapy and with appointment with behav med in 2 days. A/P Stable deeply engaged in transference. Anxiolytics seem appropriate: pt. had no CD **(Cardiac disease)** history; is very active in exploring pain rather than medicating it: and from a dynamic point of view I believe the medication represents surrogate maternal care for pt's pain. D/W **(Discuss with)** Dr. Miller Ativan 1 mg five pills Return to clinic in 3 days.

CHAPTER 12

During our afternoon walk, Beth and I discuss therapy. She is a great listener and has very insightful comments. "But no matter what you think about your therapy's quality John," says Beth, "you're learning about your emotional self, especially as a child. You're changing; you've told me so yourself, and I see it." As we wander along the country road, the facts of my case run freely through my mind. Beth is right. I'm changing, and I'm not content to leave things as they are. Her words direct my writings which lead me into the heart of my self–analysis.

Now I explore childhood feelings for my maternal grandmother, whom, except for Beth, I love the most. She is 100 years old and in the hospital with failing health. As a child her home was my safe haven. She helped clothe me, cared for me in sickness, and fed me supper every evening. Never did she speak a harsh word to me, and Grandma told me a million times how precious I was to her. "Nobody loves you more," she often said to me. Throughout life, Grandma did many pleasant things for me.

A complicated treatise could be written on my feelings for her; however, I have perpetuated my grievous self and have enthroned it at the very heart of my writing.

Day after day I told her about their violent arguments and my emotional distress, usually crying, begging, and pleading for help. I wanted her to rescue me, to make my parents stop.... I clung to Grandma for she was my last hope, the only hope; she was strong and sure and Mother did whatever she advised.

I would say with tears flooding my eyes, "My father hates me!"

Her answer was: "The Bible says you must love your father."

"But I'm afraid that he will hurt me."

"He won't hurt you. The Bible says you must honor your father. Christians learn to love. He won't hurt you. He loves you."

"But every night they fight and I cry, and they scare me. I hate them both!"

Her final word was: "Don't think of hating them because God will punish you for such thinking. Say your prayers and God will help you." The message that came through was that God didn't like a hateful, angry boy who didn't like his parents, and God would punish him accordingly.

This was the endless dialogue of a small child crying for help. One day I stopped crying for help and began to fear a God who would punish me, as my Grandmother predicted, for the evil thinking which lurked within my fantasies: I thought of killing my father or wishing him dead. And I thought that God would give me a horrible disease and hurt me or hurt the people I loved. As a child I prayed at bedtime that cancer would not strike. "Please God, protect them from cancer and all the dreadful diseases, and help them to live forty or more years...."

What kind of prayer is that for a six year old. Reading the Bible and attending Sunday School didn't help. Love, theology, and everything, it seemed, failed me, and the fear of God's wrath created a destructive and ugly force in my early life.

Later, after writing about Grandma and childhood, I deduce that both positive and negative transference feelings have created a pathway from my subconscious to conscious mind. Within this pathway suppressed feelings and memories are coming forth which, hopefully, will foster healing. Confused feelings about past love affairs and conflicts in adolescence and childhood often precede a memory. And there's a need to express myself in writing because these inner childhood conflicts, mournful and never resolved, can only be exposed this way.

Behavioral Medicine Session

Friday, Beth and I return to the hospital for my long

awaited behavioral medicine appointment. Upbeat describes our mood. Dr. Beata Kowalsky, the behavioral psychologist, arrives promptly and tells Beth she wants her to join us later. Beth waits in the reception area as Beata finds us a vacant office. "Sorry," Beata begins as we sit, "I'm on a fellowship at University and don't have an office. Dr. Fox will be joining us shortly, and he will help me with your assessment."

We socialize for a few minutes. She is from Poland, so we chat about Danzig and living in Europe—a pleasant change from Grace's staring therapy. Beata presents herself nicely, and there's an instant rapport between us.

"Why have you come to behavioral medicine?" asks Beata.

Surprised, maybe in a little shock, I answer, "Hasn't Grace spoken with you about me?"

"No she hasn't. I called her several times this week, but she hasn't returned my calls." She briefly hesitates and, then, continues in an apologetic voice, "You know how those things are. Everyone's so busy."

To Grace's defense I go, "I'm sure she sent over a consult sheet."

"No," Beata replies and opens up the folder with my name on it. "See, your folder is empty. Nothing's been sent over by Dr. Tyre. But I'll try to contact her later today." This irony brings me a deeper and less friendly understanding of Grace.

"That would be helpful," I stammer, trying to cover–up my feelings of disappointment. Next, Beata completes a lengthy fear and anxiety questionnaire. She reads me question after question and writes down my answers, much like a stenographer taking dictation. It's a slow process because Beata has difficulty understanding my English.

"I've made dramatic OCD progress," I say, "with the help of the Lord."

Beata appears surprised by my answer and replies, "That's wonderful John and quite interesting. It's good to hear your OCD has dramatically improved through your faith. Is there anything creating anxiety for you now?"

"Well," pausing, "Did you know I was in transference with Grace?"

"No," she answers, "like I said, I've no history on you."

At this time it strikes me that I shouldn't have mentioned my transference, but I go on anyway and say, "Being in transference with Grace has produced considerable anxiety." My voice seems unnaturally loud.

"Don't worry about it John!" Beata quickly replies with an air of confidence. "Your transference will eventually go away." I seem suddenly more relaxed because of Beata's confident statement.

After one and a half hours of asking questions, Beata apologizes for Dr. Fox's absence. "Dr. Fox should be here shortly," she remarks, appearing nervous.

"Did you know he sent me a letter stating he was going to meet with me?"

"Yes, I did John."

Fifteen minutes later she calls him on the phone. He tells her he will not be coming. Beata tries to convince him; he refuses. "Well then," appearing embarrassed, "can I bring Dr. Lynch to your office for just a minute to say hello?" a pause; swiftly she says again, "We'll only spend a minute, just a minute."

"Sorry John," Beata says after hanging–up, "Dr. Fox can't see you today. Perhaps, he will see you another time."

"That's OK Beata," I answer feeling peeved that the director of behavioral medicine would embarrass Beata, who seemed like a very nice, professional student.

At the end of the session Beata seems at a loss and after hesitating, she suggests, "John, will you come back for another appointment so we can finish your assessment?"

"I've got to talk with Grace first, Beata; after which, I'll make that decision." Out of curiosity I ask her, "What type of treatment will you give me?"

"You'll get a desensitization program where we give you homework assignments and you desensitize yourself to OCD fears."

"Thanks for meeting with me," I say with a smile. The session ends after two hours. I left never seeing Dr. Fox.

No record sent

Beth is annoyed when I meet her in the reception area. For two hours she has waited at Dr. Kowalsky's request.

"Why didn't she come back and get me?" Beth expresses her displeasure and, next, her concern, "I was worried and didn't know what to think."

"Everything went OK. Except," I add! "Beth, do you remember that letter where Dr. Fox said he was meeting with me?!"

"Yes."

"He refused to show up, and Beata's only a student!"

"That's very inappropriate of him," her voice echoing off the corridor walls. "Perhaps," Beth continues with a quizzical look, "he was at the party? After you left the reception area several people carried in party food trays."

As we leave the hospital I sigh, shake my head, and remark, "I'm not a patient trying to get well. To them, I'm a nuisance that they tolerate because of their economic needs."

CHAPTER 13

By now Grace is creating an antagonistic therapy, first by not calling me a name and, then, with her "staring behaviors," and, now, with her failure to provide a behavioral medicine consult or return Dr. Kowalsky's calls.

Saturday, while glancing through a book titled, *Jokes and Their Relation to the Unconscious*, I read what Freud, the author, describes as the "pleasure of nonsense" principle. Three words capture my imagination: Freud, nonsense, and pleasure. One thing I'm learning is that I may lose healing power when I limit myself. So, if Grace is just going to stare, why not create pleasurable nonsense during therapy and antagonize her like she's antagonizing me.

Creating fun in therapy is easy because creative and fantasy thinking have been part of my personality since early childhood. Why not give Grace a lecture on the "Art of Staring!" It sounds like nonsense to me, I think humorously and with a laugh. I decide to do it realizing that everything that is happening has emotional–healing potential.

Session 10/02

Usually I arrive ten minutes early for my appointment, but today in this juvenile mode I arrive exactly on time. The receptionist tells me, with a pert expression, that Grace has called for me several times; she anxiously awaits my arrival, how pleasing! After check–in I select a secluded seat which will force her to find me: my fun game of hide–and–seek. She does so shortly and with a beaming smile in silence leads me to her office.

In her office she dialogues quickly, "I'm really concerned about what happened to you at behavioral medicine. Sorry I couldn't have spoken with you longer Friday, but I was busy at home." Grace goes on, smiling once, then again, "I've just spoken with Dr. Kowalsky. See my concern for you...!"

I think carefully and, then, at her hesitation I ask, "What did she tell you?"

Grace pauses, "I won't tell you!" she answers. "It's better that you explain to me what happened Friday."

"Why didn't you take the time to write out a consult sheet or return Beata's calls?" I ask. Then I pause and hesitate, waiting for an apologetic answer. There's none, so I continue, "I showed you a lot of trust by going there," politely I say, my tone slightly metallic, "although I knew their program was standard OCD fear desensitization. You told me I didn't understand what they did. What's happening in here?" Grace's arms are now folded across her chest, exposing her iron bars against criticism. There are no apologies from her today: I'm sure of that by now. She is silent under criticism and I know why: The silent never bear witness against themselves.

After a twenty minute behavioral medicine soliloquy, it is apparent I'm getting nowhere so I hand her two pictures of myself, a baby picture and another picture of myself at four years old sitting on the Easter Bunny's lap. Grace, projecting an air of confusion, asks, "Whose lap are you sitting on?"

"Why it's the Easter Bunny," I answer, pondering if she's putting–me–on.

"Oh!" she replies placing her hand under her chin like she's made a new discovery.

"I'm tired of acting like an adult in here, so I've decided to let you meet the adolescent and child me. That's why I brought the pictures," I say while emphatically asserting, "You'll be dealing with these guys," placing the pictures on the desk, "for the next several sessions!" Her eyes glance toward them again. With the pictures now in place, I read a rather provocative quotation from Germaine Greer. By this time Grace is staring at me, intently—never blinking. A sullen little line has set about her mouth telling me she isn't going to respond.

As I start to read the quotation, "'Maybe I don't have a pretty smile, good teeth, nice tits, long legs, a cheeky arse, a sexy voice,'" her expression changes. At first she seems startled; then she seems annoyed as I continue, "'Maybe I don't know how to handle men and increase my market value, so that rewards due to the feminine will accrue to me.... I'm sick of the Powder Room...."' Grace's squinting eyes and shifting leg position tell me she's becoming angrier. "'I'm sick of pretending that some fatuous male's self–important pronouncements are the objects of my undivided attention.... I am a woman, not a castrate.'" We look at each other for several seconds, locked in a mutual incomprehension.

"Did you recognize the quote?" I ask. She shakes her head telling me no. "It's a Germaine Greer quote," quickly I say. "Interesting isn't it?"

She smiles but still refuses to break her silence which torments me, obsesses me, and confuses me. In defense, I recite a poem by Sparks which mirrors our faltering relationship: "'That old ridiculous partner is back again//who speaks my mind before me, singing me now//fonder than ever, my embarrassing vancourier//I am her fool, the nosy one to follow//years at a time, and know her for my other,//who sounds my superstition like a bagpipe//I am her acrobat....//to blow her pipes when I will dance again.' What do you think of that poem?" She refuses to speak. "Aren't you going to say anything today again?" She refuses to speak. "Well then!" I say, Grace's eyes reflecting her air of authority, power, "I'm going to give you a lecture on the art of staring. Did you know there are at least fourteen different ways to stare?" I am trying anything now to fill the session's emptiness: to make her muddy affect crystalline.

It's easy for me to lecture her, because much of my life has been spent doing it. "Take for instance," I begin, "the glare which you're doing right now. A glare's defined as a hard piercing stare which is a fixed gaze, and it indicates curiosity, boldness, and insolence. But we need to define gaze to accurately define glare." I pause, point my index finger at her and wave it like a classroom pointer. "Remember your sixth grade English rule—you can't define a word with a similar word—therefore, we need to define a gaze without using the word glare or a similar word," pausing, not wanting to lose this and the next moment of therapeutic madness.

"Gaze refers to a prolonged look that is often indicative of wonder, fascination, awe, or admiration. See, even though you think you're being insolent toward me, you're really fascinated and awed by me!"

Here I hesitate for a minute to gather my thoughts. Is there anyway to make her talk with me? Perhaps an appeal to her common sense will work. I continue in a firm tone, "All staring is a form of aggression and you know it. I'm sure you don't stare at people on the street or in a restaurant. Why are you doing it to me?!"

Grace has fixed eyes on me, but never answers. Next, I give her two examples of situations where I used staring to keep an aggressive animal at bay. When she does not respond and just keeps staring, I give her a few other examples.

Trying to relieve my tension, I occasionally recite lines from *The Taming of the Shrew*. "Say she be mute and will not speak a word//Then I'll commend her volubility//And say she uttereth piercing eloquence...."

When I pause Grace tells me the session is over. My final words to her, looking into her eyes as she stands close to me, "Do you know whom I'm referring to?" She nods her head once; then, she nods again. "By Kate," I say on my way out the door. There is no reply. As I walk down the corridor I wonder if she has begun to play terrible mind games with me and doesn't even know it.

Session 10/02 One hour psychotherapy

Patient discussed his anger at behav. medicine intake, which he described as a botched job and a failure of the organization of this department; he has many specific complaints, i.e. Dr. Kowalsky did not have her own office, did not bring his wife into session, etc. Stated that he will not return. Described Dr. Kowalsky as a "nice" otherwise unremarkable as a person. Then discussed positive transference to me—his perception of my commitment to him, my warm feelings for him; and his recent phone call with his mother, in which he felt no anger, just a sense of disengaging from her. Out to dinner with his wife/been many years, it went well. Negative suicidal ideation; negative homicidal ideation; negative psychosis.

A/P Stable and engaged. Patient was discussed with Dr. Kowalsky who agreed with patient complaints patient cited, but had felt strong rapport. My best understanding is that Dr. Kowalsky's attractiveness and intelligence were scary to patient and he has cut her off, transferring negative feelings to her and thus positive feelings to me. **(Is this believable?)** I will discuss this with Dr. Miller in supervision as I do each Monday. Continue Psychotherapy.

On our drive home Beth mentions that she has never heard of a therapy patient lecturing a therapist on staring, reciting poetry, and reading quotes.

"She's encouraging me on through silence and an occasional smile," I reply. "But I'll grant you it isn't anything like my previous therapies."

"Like I've said John, it's different than any therapy I've heard of," states Beth again, her voice sharp and clear.

CHAPTER 14

Tuesday, I purchase a joke book to keep the lecture process dynamic, for there's a certain relief in change. All the jokes in this book would be offensive to someone, I guess that's the nature of jokes. Nevertheless, I intend to select jokes that will be palatable.

As we leave the university book store Beth comments, "Do you think there's any therapeutic value in telling Grace jokes?"

"Beth," I answer, "it doesn't matter what I think because transference feelings are pulling me along. And like anyone else, I can and will take only so much staring nonsense from her."

On the way home I purchase a stuffed animal, Gonzo, one of Jim Henson's Muppets. "Grace," I tell Beth, "can learn something from this prop. Gonzo has a great therapeutic stare." Beth withholds comment as I continue explaining my therapy presentation, "Freud's writings will create the material." Immediately with a beaming look I finish, "She loves the intellectual stuff."

"John, you really have adolescent transference feelings today. There isn't any intellectual 'stuff' here," a chuckling but concerned Beth replies.

At 9 A.M. on Thursday the telephone rings. "Hello." I answer.

"My son's ill," Grace speaks, distantly, in a monotone voice, and without using my name. "Remember I told you when my child is ill I don't come to work. I'm canceling our 11 A.M. appointment. Goodbye." And she is gone.

After she hangs up I'm disrupted and sit with the phone in my hand. Why hasn't she inquired about my well being or even been polite? Grace's lack of concern creates rejection feelings which direct my writing for four consecutive days.

Self–analysis writings aren't neat and tidy, representing as they do the unresolved past conflicts of an anxious, neurotic mind searching for truth. Page after page is written on one day; then, the next day a long revision process takes place. Unresolved conflicts of my youth—sexual expressions, love feelings, and anger, churn beneath the surface of these writings.

CHAPTER 15

There's a nervous sexual undertone to my writing today, but what is happening seems inevitable. I should have known from the beginning my transference with Grace was going to force me into a sexual confrontation with her. Everything is going farther and farther awry as I write and realize that most immoral acts are undertaken with a purpose—or at least a rationalization—that is at least in part expressly moral. The wisdom of my moral appeal doesn't touch me to the quick, so I decide to explore my sexuality with her and ignore the lustful nature I'm trying to fight against. And so with this schism, of go and stop in my mind, I continue writing.

Without romantic feelings which elicit erotic feelings, what possible healing value can such an expression have? I am unsure how I feel about Grace sexually. Feelings of rebellion, anger, and love can be found, but erotic feelings are elusive. It's certainly a mystery to me and, maybe, an unsolvable one.

Later, to search for erotic feelings, I write an elaborate fantasy where we go on a secluded Alpine walk. We stroll up a mountain trail for four hours, a wonderful fall day sparkles around us. The sun is warm and its rays touch our hearts. Cows wander in the lower pastures with their bells playing a melody of love. Rolling fields covered with wind blown, blazing red poppies caress us as we stroll along. After which we eat lunch on a blanket at the snow line, a gluh wein, kase, and frische brot, und gemuse suppe.... We'll listen to an operetta, Die Das Weite, and as we listen, I'll gently give you a Shiatsu massage. Eventually we'll feel the sensuousness of our warm bodies surrounded by the cold snow....

When finished writing, I'm floundering in a quagmire of bewilderment because I have found no erotic feelings for Grace. Shortly, I commit the ultimate weakness and take a restless nap. That evening, Beth and I discuss therapy's sexual direction.

"Beth," I waver to seek the right words, "Do.... Do you think I should continue to explore my sexuality with Grace?"

"Is Grace still encouraging it?" asks Beth mildly piqued.

"Yes, she is. She's told me we're right on our sex and aggression course."

With a tear forming in her eye, Beth responds, "How will you explore sex with her?"

"It won't be much," I reply trying to minimize a troubling situation. "I've written an erotic fantasy, and I'll write her a love letter just...."

"Why would you write her a love letter?" Beth interrupts now crying. I feel suddenly overwrought and regret speaking of the matter. "You haven't written me a love letter in twenty years," Beth asserts. Her words are barely audible, but they momentarily silence me.

"Well," I flounder, putting my arm around her and carefully looking for words but finding none!

Beth slowly shakes her head before lowering her tear filled eyes and she says, "I don't think this is right! What kind of therapy are you in?!"

"How else can I find erotic feelings?" I reply hopelessly confused in nervous energy. "I'll try to leave therapy if you want me to?"

Beth answers, shaking her head and with a sigh, "It's difficult for me to deal with the thought of you having mental sex with Grace and where it could lead—but I trust you." With an expression of resolution, she goes on, "I don't want you to leave therapy!" Beth pauses and we hug as she assuredly finishes, "I want you to keep getting better. That's the most important thing!"

"Let's take a leaf peep walk," I suggest with a smile trying to escape the tension that buzzes around us. Grabbing my hand and returning my smile, Beth tells me everything is okay for now. Nevertheless, I'm running on impulse and not worrying about the ultimate.

CHAPTER 16

I once said to Grace, "I'm going to let my conscience guide me through life and therapy."

She assertively disagreed, "Do you really think your conscience can guide you anywhere?" Then answering her own question said, "It won't work." Today, I hear those warning words bouncing around in my head. In a casual, but nevertheless committed way, my conscience now directs me to think about leaving therapy.

But how to leave transference therapy is a mystery. Oh! If it could be as easy as changing physicians. Grace has told me that only she can break the bond but is this the truth? I telephone a friend with a Ph.D. in personality psychology and ask him how a transference bond is broken. "John," emphatically he states, "you're never going to cognitively explain transference emotions nor any emotion away." He tells me that his friend has been in a transference relationship for twenty years. This statement sends a chill through my body. The thought of spending twenty years reliving life's traumatic moments with my transference mother . . . horrifies me! "Some experts," he continues, "think it's only an infatuation." Although I don't respond to his comment—my transference is no infatuation—it is intense and motivates me to atypical thoughts and capricious behaviors.

Hanging up I feel a stab of alarm followed by a question: Can I develop a strategy to break my transference bond without her help? One possibility is to reconstruct her subconscious image. Grace, herself, has given me this idea by saying earlier that she will share personal feelings if I need her in an emergency. A further extension of this idea is to reformulate her image by tallying up negatives: her part–time employment status, not rescheduling appointments, failure to call me by name, and her rude affect toward Beth.... There are plenty of negatives. My final solution is to talk about the positives in my childhood and the fun side of adolescence: to alter our therapeutic perspective, as one might say.

By Saturday, Beth has been expressing distress about Grace's therapeutic methodology. Beth is a knowledgeable health care professional, who has a master's degree from the University of California at San Francisco and has completed a residency at Stanford University. Fortunately, our therapy concerns are distracted by my aunt and uncle's pending arrival from Virginia, and we both look forward to a respite from therapy "thinking."

Saturday evening my aunt and uncle arrive for a five day visit. They have known for years of my OCD. Before dinner my uncle places his used diabetic needles, which are in an old plastic coke bottle, on a coffee table very near me. Presently he says, "I'm going to give myself a shot here in the living room."

"Peter," my aunt chimes, "loves to give himself shots in front of other people."

Beth who obviously feels a sudden, powerful splash of anger says to him, "It's more appropriate to use the bathroom." Peter complies. His insensitive behavior has also made me angry and this emotion is felt as I look at the needle bottle which confronts me all evening. Later that night while sitting in a chair, he opens his shirt exposing the needle marks on his stomach. My aunt tells him he is being rude. Although I withhold comment, adrenaline floods me with anger, and I think, "Why is he acting this way? It's impolite to say the least!"

I lie in bed, now. Childhood sorrow and anger have come back to me. Remembering back to the way I had been: hurt, rejected, and lonely, forces tears to my eyes. Beth notices my extreme affect and asks, "John, what's wrong?"

"Everything's all right," I respond. "Just let me feel the emotion," my tone low, speech slowing, and words short. For more than an hour latent, neurotic hostility—childhood feelings—spontaneously break out until I'm drained of energy; then I dreamlessly sleep.

At breakfast, as I look into my aunt and uncle's faces, I

realize that my emotional bond with them has changed. Their ability to hurt me with insensitive behaviors is gone, and I don't need their love or friendship anymore. Last night I sorted through unresolved feelings toward them. Feeling their behaviors instead of listening to their words had been the key to my change. A whisper of hope is joyfully felt. If I can psychologically change my relationship with my aunt and uncle, perhaps, it can be done with Grace.

Session 10/09

Grace sits smiling and says, "I want you to know that missing sessions is a good thing. It's your psychological checkup." Checkup for what? Her words leave me perplexed.

"That's all right," I answer. "How's your son?"

"He's fine, it was just a cold. Aren't you the least bit angry at me for missing last session? Didn't you feel rejected even though I couldn't help missing?"

"No, I didn't," I reply with two hurried shakes of my head and think, "Why complain and waste time! Nothing will change! Grace's behavior is so much like Mother's it's uncanny. They both use a controlling friendliness to mitigate their responsibility to others. Grace with her light patient load should be rescheduling my appointments because transference relationships are special and need to be treated as such, and Grace, like Mother, gets more pleasure using manipulative control than from empathetic compliance."

I take Gonzo from a bag, place him on my lap, and say in a pleasant, challenging tone, "I've a special joke presentation for you. Doesn't Gonzo have an interesting therapeutic stare? Better than the one you use every week." Grace crosses her legs than recrosses them, cocks her head slightly, and stares back at Gonzo who effectively counters her stare. Next, I hand her my typed introduction which she takes and silently reads as I remark, "All performers need a good introduction. Would you read mine?"

"No!" she answers bitingly, leaning back in her chair once again. "You'll have to read it yourself if you want it read."

Carefree adolescent feelings are flowing, so I come back

with a slight laugh before saying, "I don't mind reading it at all. It might be better if I do." With my voice now raised to higher pitch I nervously begin, "With enormous enthusiasm, unsinkable optimism, and a streak of inspired lunacy.... John the great.... And now for the presentation."

Grace interrupts and asks in a stage whisper, "Should I laugh at your jokes?"

"Do whatever you want. But don't forget you told me I couldn't laugh in therapy." She mimics her usual therapeutic posture and stares. Once again, her eyes are never blinking, in sharp contrast to my first therapist who rapidly blinked his eyes to keep me talking. A different subliminal technique, I suspect.

My performance is not stellar by any account. Throughout the performance I am self–conscious and detect, perhaps, the insecurity of a teenage boy telling jokes to a girl. "Grace, what was Amelia Earhart's big problem?—She didn't go all the way." She laughs slightly with a nervous undertone as I go on, my voice quavering, "What song did the lovesick shepherd sing?—There'll never be another ewe." She semismiles at this joke, catches herself, and returns to that stern gaze I know so well. After six or seven jokes, I recognize her indication of displeasure: her posture has become rigid, her look incredulous.... Now I, take a deep breath and continue with a series of jokes to sense her attitude toward men. These jokes have been constructed only with the startling intent of arousing emotion in her.

"How do Yale men define foreplay with a Yale woman?—Begging and pleading.

What's a 10,9,8,7,6,5,4,3,2,1?—Grace getting older.

After 7 years of therapy, Dr. Lynch is prepared to go it alone:

'Grace,' he asks quite confidently, 'will you do me one big, big favor before I leave?' 'If I can,' she cordially replies. 'Grace, will you give me a goodbye kiss before I leave?' 'Why John,' Grace replies quite firmly, 'you know the rules, remember our therapeutic fence.' But John will not give up and says, 'Can't you break a rule this once?' 'Absolutely not John, Why, I shouldn't even be on the couch with you!!'"

There's a cool, concernless silence between us here as I try, but fail, to sense what she's feeling.

"Do you want me to finish my presentation?" I ask. She smiles weakly and shrugs her shoulders, her yes answer.

"Here's your homework assignment for next session," I go on to say: "First I want you to explain Freud's concept of the *Pleasure of Nonsense*! Next, you are to identify each of my jokes according to Freud's tendentious joke classifications." And finally, I read her a Freudian quote knowing she won't like it: "'The power which makes it difficult or impossible for women to enjoy undisguised obscenity is termed repression which may keep whole complexes of impulses, together with their derivatives, away from the consciousness causing a psychoneuroses.' I want you to explain why your inability to laugh at my obscene jokes shouldn't be considered as a sign of a severe psychoneurosis in you, as Freud suggests?'"

"Do you know that jokes are a form of aggression?" she snaps, her voice like a whiplash. Her face is contorted with anger.

"To me, jokes represent whatever the joker and jokee think they represent." I counter, lounging indolently back in the chair. Nevertheless, for my part, I'm saying indirectly to her, "Listen to me, I am rebelling against your rejections."

"You're only telling me jokes because I've canceled our last session!" rebuts Grace, her voice becoming raised, defining the arrogance of pride between us. She is obviously wrong about the reason but partially right if she's inferring rebellious motivation.

The telephone rings; she answers it and talks for a minute. Once she's finished I comment, "No more jokes today." Then, lingering and fixing my eyes on her, I say, "I want to explore my erotic feelings toward you—it's time." I linger again to capture her look and make sure her eyes are telegraphing approval. "I'll do it next week if that's okay?" Never wavering, she nods her head once in approval; then she nods again. Her nods and eyes for the briefest moment have made it clear that she has made an offer, as unmistakable as anything I've ever seen. "I'd like you to wear the following turn–ons for me," I direct, my voice low, smooth and, then, I continue, "You know, we need to create the right erotic atmosphere in here. How about wearing your sienna cowgirl boots! You've a 'fine' cowgirl look, and they go nicely with your black print dress. Also, wear those gold hoop earrings you wore for your supervisor's meeting...." When I finish I know what she will do. Grace will wear her sienna cowgirl boots and the long dress but not the earrings. Her affect now transmit's much to me!

"How are you controlling your feelings toward me?" I inquire later in a low brash tone.

"My feelings for you are controlled," she answers swiftly, her words tumbling out one over the other. Her voice still raised as she continues, "There's been only one instance, our romantic walk, during therapy, and I've apologized for suggesting that you were sexually aroused!"

I jest, "Only one!" a raised eyebrow telling her what she has said isn't true....

At this later point I explain what has happened during my aunt and uncle's visit. After listening to my description, Grace comments inditingly, "Your uncle is a sadistic person." Her sweeping condemnation of what is surely insensitive, but hardly sadistic, behavior on my uncle's part seems uncalled for. Grace who knows nothing about him indites him again, "He just did it because he knew you had OCD and wanted to hurt you. That's why!" Discontent crosses my face, and I shrug my shoulders when she finishes, realizing that she has no clue about our forty year relationship. What purpose can she have for encouraging me to sever family relationships? We sit silently for a minute or so, having locked in a mutual incomprehension.

Eventually I remark, "Beth thought of calling you about my regressive emotional behavior." Grace gives no response, so I give up, and we sit, once again, for a long time in silence.

Finally, Grace breaks the silence and suggests, "We need to strengthen our therapeutic relationship." Aggressively I snap, "Why would I want to strengthen my relationship with you!" I am still angry that she offered no advice regarding my emotional regressions and about her sadistic profile of my uncle, a kind man at heart. It is unfair to say I do not want a better relationship with her, but I sense by now she really doesn't want one. My therapist, it seems, is all "smoke and mirrors" about creating a better relationship. Therapy may just be some kind of mental game to her; perhaps, I think, that's what therapy really is. No more words are spoken and the session ends.

Session 10/10 One hour psychotherapy (Wrong date)
Patient discussed his experience with visit from uncle who has IDDM **(Diabetes)** and used needles in patient's living room and presence; this precipitated another powerful sense of regression in the pt. to childhood emotions, which he was able to tolerate and recover from with a new understanding of his uncle as a deeply cruel man. Also demonstrated, but did not acknowledge anger at therapist; was able at the end of the session to discuss his feelings around my cancellation last week. Affect full, congruent. TC **(Thought control/content)**; negative suicidal ideation; negative homicidal ideation; negative psychosis. A/P Stable, tolerating emotions aroused by family and able to tolerate therapists absence. Return to clinic 3 days.

On the way home I talk, and Beth listens. "The only thing I'm sure of," I assert to Beth, "is that my challenge to her therapeutic staring has annoyed her and something will change." Further, I declare, "Nothing good is going to come from all this rejection, especially when I have all these transference feelings toward her. Perhaps now, through rebellious behaviors, I have convinced her that staring will not work." Sudden revulsion seizes me, disgust, loathing for her whole therapeutic style, and I ask myself about healing, "Is it worth this? more than this? or nothing at all?"

By the next evening, Beth and I are hopelessly confused

and exhausted from therapy's stress. Beth comments as we search for answers, "John, I've read that poorly administered transference therapies can lead to vengeful therapeutic relationships. Why don't I acquire information from Janet?" Janet, Beth's friend, is a psychiatric nurse practitioner and has been working in mental health for more than twenty years. She has done 200 psychiatric evaluations, mental status exams, and is married to a board certified psychiatrist.

Beth and Janet talk for quite a while about our therapy concerns; then, Janet and I begin to talk.

After we talk for a bit, I ask Janet if she has ever heard of a therapeutic technique by which a therapist refuses to call a patient by name.

She responds laughing like I have told her a joke. Swiftly Janet catches herself and in a more serious tone says, "What do you mean?"

"My therapist," I answer, "doesn't call me by name before, during, or after the session, and even when we speak on the telephone."

Janet responds incredulously, "Oh! My goodness! What does she call you?"

I answer, "Nothing!" As I say this I feel rejected and angry with myself for continuing therapy. I'm not a "nothing," swallowing hard I think. We talk for over an hour, and Janet's information suggests, like Beth's, that there is something wrong with my therapy, if in fact it is therapy.

Today as I drive to therapy, the thought of having mental sex with another woman troubles me from the bottom of my stomach to the top of my throat. I'm feeling, in about equal parts—lust and guilt. Both of these feelings attach themselves to Beth and Grace. In the reception area, I whimsically write on a slip of paper, cowgirl boots and black print dress.

Session 10/12

Grace arrives resplendent in her cowgirl boots and black print dress. We stand looking at each other for several seconds. Tension buzzes as she hugs my shoulder and glances at me on our walk to her office. Once seated, she crosses her

legs and, then, lifts her dress to give me a clear view of her
boots. While she measures my reaction, I casually notice she
hasn't worn her gold hoop earrings because her hair has been
uncharacteristically pulled back. I know I ought to say
something erotic to her now, but at the moment it seems
impossible, so I say instead, "I'm not going to have mental
sex with you today; I've changed my mind," and hand her the
slip of paper.

She unfolds the paper and reads it. Her outward
appearance changes instantly and she is angry, very angry.
She explodes once, "Why the hell do you think I would 'dress
up' for you!!!" Then again, "I wouldn't 'dress up' for you;
who the hell do you think you are!!!!" There's a long, uneasy
pause between us, and I wonder for a horrible moment what
I have done. She mutters in a low voice more to herself than
to me, "Why are you doing this to me?" An eon of silence
falls. With injured dignity she continues, "I wear boots all the
time. What makes you think I picked them out especially for
you. Why are you doing this to me?!"

This rather dreadful thought comes to mind, I have no
idea what horrible thing I have done. I hesitate drained of
thought but still impulsively answer, "I wanted to cause you
a dilemma." Her hands tighten on the chair, and contempt
comes into her eyes. By now, I realize it has been a mistake
to hand her this note but, still, I do not suspect the written
words are at fault.

The session is chaotic and it's my fault. Grace is angry
and postures herself rigidly waiting for me to speak, and I
want to be anywhere else in the world but in this crazy room.
"Our relationship is too chaotic," I say in appeal to break the
silence. "Our chaotic minds have yoked themselves together
like I've already told you."

"Tell me how it's chaotic?!" she snaps, her voice loud, her
eyes blazing. It's an incongruent question because this session
is proving it, at least to me.

"Two minds," I continue selecting my words carefully,
"can interlock in a way where each finds pleasure in creating

emotional chaos for the other...." Grace tips her head to the side, her face a mirror of disarray, always silent, her eyes flaring. "Much of this chaos is my fault, and I want to be a better patient."

"I've enjoyed watching your childish behavior during the past few sessions. It's been quite insightful," Grace finally speaks. Her tone is unmistakably cold and sarcastic.

Right now I reason that she is falling deeper and deeper into her emotional self. I know her better, perhaps than any other being does and that's what's scaring her and me. So to refocus her I say, "Beth is upset at you."

"Why?" Grace drawls, draws herself up, and recrosses her legs. A petulant line has set about her mouth.

"Because you never acknowledge her in the reception area." I pause and wait for a reply. Her unresponsiveness angers me so I continue, snapping, "And she's also jealous because you dressed up for me," pausing, watching her, "and you've been encouraging me sexually!" My voice drifts off, tired. There is an awful silent pause, than an irrepressible snicker from her as she intently watches for my reaction. I'm vacillating between bitterness and mental exhaustion and decide not to participate in the terrible mind game she's playing. Instead, I enter her screaming silence and hide my anger. Eventually, her unrelenting stare unnerves me, and I protect my weakened self with sheerly nervous, defensive, remarks.

"Are you absolutely sure you're controlling your countertransference?"

"I told you last session that I'm a well–trained professional and know how to conduct therapy. Why do you keep asking me?" a darkness of discontent lies across her face.

"It's hard to believe. That's why!" hesitating, " and you mean there has only been one recognized instance of counter–transference in over twenty sessions?" Her cold authoritative stare transmits—I only have to answer those questions I want to. And that's how it goes for awhile with me; I am feeling worse every minute....

"What do you think about my therapeutic concerns?" I ask toward the session's end.

She starts to speak but, then, restrains herself and replies, "I'll have to think about them."

"Why are you trying to make me angry by refusing to discuss my concerns?" quickly I respond. "Don't you realize at some point if you continue this behavior I'm going to aggressively fight back."

She shakes her head teasingly, as if she has been scolding me. Shortly, her shoulder shrug and smile tell me that she seems pleased, perhaps delighted at the session's outcome.

Grace looks at the clock. "Your time's up," she says.

"Why is she so pleased?" I wonder. As I walk out the door her now soft voice calls out sarcastically, "Good–bye, Dr. Lynch." My thought in the corridor develop a master plan, break the bond, and escape this craziness.

Session 10/12 One hour psychotherapy Ativan 0.5–1mg prn (Wrong date/her notes confused)

Patient discussed his need to control transference, and his feeling that he has ended it by provoking me to show annoyance. Also discussed criticisms of the therapist, but stated therapist has helped him greatly. Said he has realized that his aggression is not as bad as he feared and might even be seen as humorous by some. Has used less than 5 mg Ativan to date.

A/P Discuss with Dr. Miller. Stable. No acting out. Continues in transference but with concerns over loss of control. I have considered decreasing intensity of therapy but given patient's stability, progress, and the likelihood that he would perceive this as an unwarranted rejection, will continue dynamic work—but will remind patient, if he brings up loss of control again, that he can elect to decrease number of sessions.

That evening I lay awake thinking as my mind jumps around. Finally moved by some desperate instinct, I can't keep away from it and think solely about ending therapy.

The next morning Beth mentions that her readings of last

night suggest a therapist should always be neutral, but she qualifies the statement by asking, "John, have you ever heard of the term Borderline Personality Disorder?"

"No. Why do you want to know?"

"Giovacchini's book on transference mostly discusses BPDs, and he tells about their transference psychoses. But he never defines BPD characteristics."

"Sorry," I reply and go on, "I've never heard of BPD, but psychosis sure isn't a good word."

"John!" Beth later adds another worry, "The famous psychiatrist Karen Horney has written that if a caring therapeutic alliance isn't established an alternate vengeful one might emerge." This is a disconcerting thought, so I banish it to the recesses of my mind.

Saturday, my writings go like this: Grace has failed me throughout my therapy, of course, but she has never been mean or nasty toward me until now. Her chaotic aggression and nastiness in Thursday's session have given me a chance to see her in a different light, to redefine her and, maybe, break the bond.... My mother was never overtly nasty to me.

By Monday, heading for therapy, I haven't gotten her out of my mind. Nervous, worrying, I heed the warning words of Tsvetaeva, "A deception that elevates me is dearer than a host of lower truths."

Session 10/16

Grace sits and smiles at me. I hand her my journal and review it. My voice seems unnaturally loud as I speak. "Your behavior toward me last session has broken my transference bond. I'm out of transference!"

She seems perplexed, leans forward in her chair, a shadow of discontent crosses her face. "What makes you think so?" she asks.

"Well, you caused it by being mean to me last session and especially when you said, 'Why the hell would I dress up for you!'" Her look goes blank, and I wonder for one horrible moment if....

"Did I say that?" she replies, startled, her eyes big and her mouth slightly open.

"Yes you did say it and several times," I answer.

She looks at me watchful, guarded, but doesn't speak. Her confused affect is so different that it arouses feelings of concern in me. "I want you to know you're really helping me," capriciously I remark, my voice steady.

"That's nice to know. I'm trying."

"I'm on the healing road."

"That's nice to know."

"Also, I realize my transference has been difficult on both of us and...."

Grace uncharacteristically interrupts and asks with no particular expression, "Would you tell me about all the mistakes I've made?" I sit there for a moment, surprised, watching her, unsure of what words to use. An instinct tells me to highlight criticism carefully for fear of upsetting her.

"Well," I begin, "First there's...."

When I'm done she leans slightly sideward in her chair, puts her hand under her chin, and asks, "Is it hard to deal with such a lousy therapist who has made so many mistakes?" Her mouth suddenly twists into a smile.

Grace's sheath of external impermeability appears to be weakening—she's overreacting to mild criticism, so I hurriedly answer, "At least you tried new things," but I don't have any idea what "new things" means except her therapy has been exceedingly different from prior ones.

"How did you feel about your other therapists?"

"I've told you all this before."

"Would you tell me again?"

"Sure, my first therapist was.... I had good relationships with them, but they didn't help my OCD."

"Tell me about your OCD progress." She hasn't inquired about my OCD progress for months.

"My progress is great," I answer, smiling, pointing to my tennis shoes, while feeling a twitch of suspicion about her sudden interest. "I'm currently confronting some very high–level OCD fears. Still, childhood fear conditioning is a stumbling block at times. For instance, I went to my dentist to have a tooth repaired and during the visit, I saw blood around the cuspidor. It made me quite anxious, so I asked the dentist to wipe it off and change gloves. Rather than being angry, he became upset and apologetic...."

"Things like this also make me nervous," replies Grace. "Sorry, but your time is up." She stands; then she says, her eyes sharp with interest, "The session's over but I want to ask if you feel integrated as a person?"

"Sure I am," quickly I reply as this dreadful thought comes to mind—I don't know whether I am or not. Trying to keep my voice steady, I inquire of her, "Don't you think I'm integrated?"

Her answer, a fleeting smile.

Walking down the corridor I realize, I haven't gotten the slightest piece of her out of mind. Youthfully addictive feelings of love, anger, sadness, and foolishness are refelt through her, those things I most and least want to feel and remember as an adult attach me to her. Disgusted with myself, I think, "Oh! Will it never end!"

Session 10/16 One hour psychotherapy (This record is changed, it was a Monday session not a Thursday session)
Patient presented on time as usual; however, I was delayed ten minutes and patient states my message was not relayed to him. Patient again focused on sexualized aggression, with strong transference to therapist; expression was appropriate without acting out. Patient plans attendance at concert this weekend. A/P Continues stable Tolerating transference. Discuss with Dr. Miller in supervision Return to Clinic three days.

CHAPTER 17

At 6 P.M. this evening I'm overwhelmed with anxiety, so I lie down on my bed. Immediately, sobs and words rush from my subconscious mind: "I tried so hard for you to love me; I've done everything. Why won't you love me? What's wrong with me, God?" How lonely and desperate I seem to myself. Later that evening I feel better. Latent emotion has come up and created healing.

The next morning a disconcerting thought comes to mind; perhaps, there's no core person within me, only free–floating personality parts. Thoughts of "this" me and "that" me return.

On our daily walk I tell Beth, "From a therapeutic standpoint to integrate myself, the only thing that makes sense is to bring forth all that subconscious, verbal, adolescent aggression like Grace wants—to take every ounce of her healing medication."

"How are you going to do it?" asks Beth quizzically.

"I'll be verbally obnoxious to her. If I can cloak my conscience enough to find latent emotions, I may be able to see beyond her rejection and discover who I really am. There was plenty of free–floating aggression in my teenage self and if this aggression surfaces as transference feelings...." Our discussion ends as I solely need the quiet time. But, eventually, I go on, "If it wasn't for this transference bond and my desire to heal at almost any cost, you know, I would have already left her." There is sorrow now as I realize that things may not come quietly and smoothly to an end between Grace and me. My words drift to hope—somewhere else a warm sun still shines and flowers are still in bloom.

As the day wears on, my mind obsesses from one point of logic to another and gives me no rest at all. There's a sense of injury from Grace which progresses to consternation and, then, to incredulity which turns to chagrin.

That afternoon, Beth waits in a grocery store check–out line while I mill around a fruit isle. Suddenly, an interesting thought pops to mind—what fun it would be to throw the fruit around the store with a friend: have a quick game of catch. Leaving the store, I see a flattened pile of garbage in the parking lot. "What the f— is that!" I bellow out. Emotions from my youth have surfaced; Beth can't believe my changed affect and language. A man in the parking lot hears me, too, and he starts laughing.

For several days adolescent emotions flow in a brilliant, awesome fashion and the emotional freedom of thirty–five years ago motivates me. I treat Beth like a teenage girlfriend, constantly holding her hand and randomly kissing her.... She enjoys the novelty of my youthful behavior which brings out lighthearted feelings in her, too.

Before therapy I spend several hours making myself angry at Grace. As I walk down the hospital corridor, the following thoughts are running through my mind like a mantra: "Tell her to go f— herself, break the bond, and find yourself."

Session 10/19

Grace is prompt, but still there have been those agonizing, long minutes waiting for it all to start. She greets me with a smile; I greet her with a glare. In her office I toss my journal on her desk and say, "I'll keep the time during the session. I'm sick and tired of you rejecting me with this 'time thing.'"

She's startled and replies, "What are you doing? What's going on?"

"Just act like a f—in' therapist for a change and try to figure it out. I'll tell you during the last ten minutes of the session." Her office computer faces me, flashes colors, and beeps. "Aren't you going to turn that computer off; it's annoying me!" I demand.

She looks at it, her eyes blazing in power, and retorts, "No, I'm going to leave it on! "

There's a short silence. "You know, I thought for two hours last night about having sex with you but decided sex with a younger woman would be more fun. Anyway, you have small tits...." Her icy stare fuels my anger. I continue to insult and swear at her. The words don't matter; they aren't real anyway.

As the session unfolds the computer flashes, she stares, and I talk obnoxiously to her. Then, not unexpectedly, the phone rings and interrupts the session. Interruptions have occurred in at least a third of our sessions. Grace answers it, talks for a minute, and says, "You'll have to excuse me. Dr. Picker, the person I share my office with, wants to pick up several records."

"Now I know why you left the f—in' computer on," cuttingly I reply; then I add, "because he left it on." There's a knock at the door. Grace goes into the hallway and shuts the door behind her.

Although I feel angry with her, I also feel the need to protect her, too, and I say on her return, "Listen, he has f—ed you over at least five times that I've seen. I don't give a f— about me, but I don't like him f—in' you over." Her swimming eyes look toward me with hate, hot anger floating in them as I continue, "In all my previous therapies, I've never had a session interrupted. What's going on here? Why is he constantly interrupting our sessions...?!" A nerve has been struck because she knows the therapy session is a sanctuary and this guy is taking advantage of her.

"Who's trying to make you feel small?" Her question to change subjects.

"Who's making you feel small?" she repeats.

"Who the f— cares!" I reply, hovering just above emotional exhaustion.

"Is it your mother or grandmother?"

"How come you don't like to talk about f—in' me?! I thought that's what my therapy was all about?"

"I'll be glad to talk about f—in' you anytime, but this is about aggression," she replies. Exhausted, drained suddenly of emotional energy and cognitive thought, I lapse into wordlessness.

By now much childhood and teenage aggression has been released. A minute later my anger is gone and my thoughts have been gathered. So I calmly say, still feeling cold and unsure on the inside, "This is how I'm working out my adolescent aggression." When Grace doesn't respond, I express my concern by asking, "Are you certain all this aggression and these insulting remarks toward you are appropriate?"

"Yes! We're both rugged and can take this kind of therapy," she answers supportively. "You're doing the right thing, and we're on the right track." Nevertheless, tension crackles across the four feet that separate us. The session ends.

Session 10/19 One hour psychotherapy
Patient yet more explicit and aggressive with sexual and aggressive imagery. Limited insight; was able to see that sex for him has been means of expressing rage, belittlement of female. Requested new Ativan script, also Tylenol IV for chronic back pain (uses very infrequently), has used minimal Ativan, with relief. O: Mood okay, affect superficial coy, frequent swearing.

A/P Stable, engaged in therapy; difficulty with modulating affect at this point, but still no safety/acting out issues. Ativan 1 mg tabs number 30 Tylenol IV number 12. **(Wrong amount)** Return to clinic three days.

On the way home, I tell Beth how therapy went and remark, "Grace said that swearing behavior has been perfectly appropriate, and we are both rugged enough to manage it. But I still worry about what good all this aggression is going to do...!"

Beth responds with a look of worry as I think of a poem I gave Grace:

> Most that I know but one
> Make me better than I am,
> Freer and more intent,
> Glad and more indolent
> What shall I think of you,
> Who makes me worsen?
> Is it hate I have,
> And if so, what is hate

That makes me reprobate
By expectation?
Or do learn your lack,
Not mine and give it back
As mine, the empty lack as mine
That makes me worsen?
And if you do misread
Me in your own need,
Why do I care whose is
The botched lesson?
Because I think if one
Should bring to mind my disdain
So near destruction,
I think that it should be
Crying out, Help me!
Help me. (Miles)

That evening Beth and I attend a piano recital at University College and drink a few glasses of wine. On the way home from the recital, Beth comments, "John, I'm amazed at how much you've begun to enjoy music."

I reply, "Music's a very healthy tranquilizer, Beth. It evokes good feelings and thoughts."

Today, I receive a $240 bill from the behavioral medicine department. The bill lists Dr. Bower as the provider at $120 an hour and Dr. Kowalski as a student at $0 per hour. I never met Dr. Bower, and Beata never mentioned him.

On the session morning, my emotional adrenalin is flowing like it always did before I played an important tennis match. Sitting in the reception area, I ominously reflect on Congreve's warning words: "Heaven has no rage like love to hatred turned...!"

Session 10/23

Grace appears annoyed, agitated, and angry as we enter her office: my feelings exactly. No words are minced as I say, "You were f—in' rude to me to leave that computer on last week."

She snaps back in an angry voice, "You can say as many f—s' in therapy as you want, but you're not to swear at me. I can't stand it! I just can't stand it!!" Her shrill tone, ringing with indignation.

I'm angry but instantly stop swearing. "You've told me over and over that I can say anything in here. Last session when I swore you said it was the right thing to do. In fact, you said we were both rugged enough to take it. Your behavior is again chaotic! Why didn't you call and tell me this before the session....?!" Adrenaline flows from nervous energy.

"I was too busy. It makes me uncomfortable and the fence changes anytime I want it to, that's it. You can swear all you want in therapy but not at me!" Her mouth twists in temper.

I shrug off her anger, throw the behavioral medicine bill on the desk, and say, "I'm being billed by someone who never saw me and according to you never wrote a record."

"The bill's perfectly correct. What do you think of that?!"

"Who cares about the bill, anyway. I'm more aggravated at you for leaving the computer on last session."

"Wouldn't your mother have left it on?!"

"No, my mother didn't spend her day thinking up ways to anger me!"

"Even if it was your father's data?"

"She would have turned it off. My mother cared for me in a lot of ways."

There's a long time of silent staring during which her face is as cold as ice, and I find myself collapsing under the weight of her wrath. I drift into a state of bewilderment and ask myself, "Why have I acted so horribly?"

"I'm going to leave," I now say and add, "There's too much craziness in here for me. You've changed everything again and created it." As I stand I desperately hope she will say something like, "Let's sit and talk about our therapeutic relationship," or that she will even encourage me to finish the session. By now, her stare has become one of sardonic pleasure as she senses my pitiable state. She makes no comment as I open the door and leave.

A mortal blow has been delivered from the last person I expected to hurt me. For a few minutes I wander around the lobby looking for Beth. When I find her, she settles me down and encourages me to return and talk with Grace.

In Grace's office again, her forgiveness for my rude behavior is sought, "I desperately want to form a better therapeutic relationship with you!" I begin with my nerves throbbing as I speak.

"We don't have any relationship!" she snaps, her tone distant. "This is only about you." Her attempt to deeply hurt me succeeds—I shut down verbally, not sure what to do or say as she watches my reaction. Feelings of rejection from childhood surge: time and space are naught. She never speaks, only stares, as I desperately try to connect with her while defending my weakened self.

"You don't know who I am as a person. If you did you would never have led me into all this sex and aggression craziness.... I've always hated any form of verbal aggression and swearing—it brings back horrible memories from my childhood and memories of the time I swore at the first girl I loved when, after driving three hours for a date, she told me about a new boyfriend...!" I feel helpless and alone as I continue, my stomach heaving, and my hands cold, "We've developed a relationship exactly like my parents. My mother annoys my father. He swears at her. And she gets even with him by rejecting him."

Grace speaks only to say, "The session's over."

As we stand I ask her, "Please give me your supervisor's name. I've had enough of this madness."

"No, you can't have his name!" firmly she rebuts.

"You have to tell me. It's my right as a patient," I counter.

"I don't have to tell you anything!" Grace rebuts again.

I leave the office and find Beth in the psychiatry reception area waiting nervously for me. After I tell her Grace won't give me her supervisor's name, Beth asks the receptionist. She doesn't know. We leave the hospital.

Session 10/23 One hour psychotherapy

Patient today enraged regarding bill from Behav. Medicine, demanded "apology," loud swearing—no obvious error in bill at all and certainly not appropriate for this therapist to apologize: none given—increased swearing. Patient redirected not to swear at therapist; walked out of session, then returned after about 10 minutes. Calmer, but angry regarding limit setting; repeated denigration of therapist's competency and judgment. Attended concert this weekend.

O: Emphatic, slightly threatening gestures turning to agitation speech loud and rapid, becoming shout. Thought process logical and coherent. Thought content negative suicidal ideation; negative homicidal ideation; negative audiovisual hallucinations; negative delusions. Assessment/Plan positive for acting out in session boundary set and complied with, although patient unable to acknowledge need for boundary; he ended session with strong narcissistic defenses, which I attempted to bolster by heavy praise for patient's work. Discussed as usual with Dr. Miller, who feels work is going well—testing and establishment of boundaries acting to create increasingly predictable and safe environment, but with patient showing increased distress as defenses come into conflict with his need for intimacy with therapist. Patient continues safe, functioning fairly well outside sessions i.e. attending concert—new exposure.

Beth drives me home. I feel desperate and wonder if I've helplessly witnessed my own destruction. "What have I done? Why have I allowed Grace to carry me into such trauma? Will Grace harm me psychologically when I'm so emotionally vulnerable?"

"Dr. Tyre has taken you away from yourself by encouraging behavior that appears atypical to me. And these behaviors are frightening you," says Beth, supportively and encouragingly near home. Nevertheless, as we turn into our driveway, I am experiencing an irritating nausea throughout my body.

At 2 P.M. I call Grace. She calls me back at 5:30 P.M.. Her voice is cold and detached.

"You're doing fine."

"But I'm distraught over what's happened in therapy today."

"Don't worry about it. Take a long walk, a couple of tranquilizers, and go to bed."

"I'm really distraught and depressed about therapy," I insist hoping to be heard, feeling wavelike contractions in my stomach.

"Listen, it's late and I have to go home. We can talk more on Thursday."

"I need to talk with you for a few minutes," my voice shutting down. When she doesn't answer, I say weakly, "Can you give me the emergency room number?"

"It's..., but let me tell you how it works. We only see people for ten minutes in the ER, and you'll have to wait hours for this ten minute meeting."

"What about the emergency clinic tomorrow?"

"It can take days to schedule you there. Forget about it! Listen, I have to go. Goodbye." And she is gone.

After hanging up, I tell Beth what Grace has said. Beth replies, "She's lying to you. Emergency rooms and emergency clinics don't operate this way and Grace—Dr. Tyre—knows it. We've had enough of this madness! You're going to the emergency room, immediately!"

I call the emergency room. A nurse answers the ER phone and tells me the on–call psychiatrist is on the phone. "He'll call you back as soon as he hangs–up," she says.

Fifteen minutes later Dr. Barber calls. He counters my concerns by repeatedly saying, "There's no reason for you to come into the ER. Don't come!" Hurriedly he adds, "Why don't you write in your journal. That will help you cope."

A red flag goes up! My journal hasn't been mentioned to him. "Have you spoken with Dr. Tyre about me?" I inquire.

"No! I haven't been on the phone all night," he quickly asserts. Our conversation ends with him refusing to see me.

Beth is angry. "We'll see about that," she says and calls the ER. "I'm right, the charge nurse has said, 'That's not how the ER is run at University. If your husband wants to be seen, he'll be seen!' Let's go!"

Beth has to drive me to the emergency room. Instinct and experience tell me that something is very wrong with my therapy and that my journal must be read at all cost. Beth holds my hand and comforts me in the reception area. I'm overwrought in a morass of emotional confusion, wondering if I'm crazy. After waiting an hour Beth asks if we can sit in a private ER room. Sitting there, Dr. Tyre's words keep flashing in my mind: "I'll be there when you need me, day or night." I need her now, but where is she? Beth and I see another psychiatrist who has come in for a patient. Where's my therapist?

Emergency Room Visit 10/23

An hour later the on–call psychiatrist, Dr. Barber, arrives. I tell him that Dr. Tyre's therapy is chaotic. "Why don't you find another therapist?" he suggests and explains, "There's a very good psychodynamic therapist in Norwood." It's an expedient answer and odd comment because there are thirty–three other psychiatrists in the hospital's practice—why send me to Norwood? unless....

"I'm in transference with Grace so that's impossible," distraughtly I answer.

"Why don't you go back and work it out with her?" he encourages.

"I've been trying for months to straighten out my therapy, but it's been madness in there.... Grace told me at a session's end that I might start cutting myself with a knife," hesitating from nervousness and going on, "that's all she said.... And she won't even call me by name." Dr. Barber looks startled but doesn't respond.

"What do you want me to do?" he asks.

"I requested Grace's supervisor's name so he could read my journal, but she wouldn't tell me."

"I don't believe that," he contradicts me, his voice sure.

"My therapy journal needs to be read."

"Well, I don't know if someone will read it."

Beth hurriedly interjects an appeal, "I've known John for

twenty–seven years, and I've never seen him like this. He has never been a psychiatric emergency patient, even in his worst OCD period. I expect something to be done!"

"I need to be stabilized," I timidly demand, my voice low.

His pager goes off. "Excuse me," he says and leaves the room.

On returning his affect is noticeably changed. "I'll take your journal to Dr. Tyre's supervisor. He'll read it and give you assistance." He asks, "Do you want an appointment in the emergency clinic tomorrow?"

"Yes," I answer not wanting my situation to be forgotten. He shakes my hand, calls me by name, and we leave. Dr. Barber has met with us for over an hour. In the corridor my mind empties of courage and lapses back into renewed worry.

Emergency Room Visit 10/23 Arrival Time: 19:35

Chief Complaint: Psychiatric Dr. Lynch presents to ED to discuss the "regression in the transference" with his therapist, Grace Tyre, M.D. over past months. He feels that he has become "unstable" in therapy with her. He has been seen for OCD and now exploratory therapy. Patient was accompanied by wife, who appears supportive. He describes things as "came to a head" today and needs to be seen to be restabilized. Psychiatric history and psychotherapy.

Meds: none MSE (mental status exam)—Neatly dressed, mildly disheveled hair, clean, good eye contact; normal speech; no abnormal behaviors; mood "unstable" affect—constricted, intense. Thought process: linear coherent; no evidence of psychotic signs and symptoms; judgment/insight–intact Patient denies suicidal and parasuicidal ideation. Assessment: Fifty–year old man who has developed intense transference to current therapist. He is concerned about the intensity and feels that he needs to stop therapy but wants supervisor's input to therapeutic process.

Plan: 1. Supportive reality–based interaction. 2. Contact Dr. Grace Tyre concerning patient's condition, concerns. 3. Present information to Dr. Tyre's supervisor for review. 4. Contract for safety. 5. Patient will be seen in AM through Crisis and Brief Therapy Service.

Diagnosis: OCD; Adjustment Disorder Assessment and

Diagnosis (DSM III R)—Adjustment Disorder Plan and Disposition: Discharge Home D.J. Barber Jr., MD

Early Tuesday morning I write intensely: "Someone must help me leave transference and deal with these confused emotions.... I guess these writings must be ended—they have only contributed to my therapeutic disaster, not helped me get better.... My dream to heal is dead. Even Grace can't accept me.... I am probably just insane...."

Session 10/24

Later, Beth and I go to the crisis clinic. Overwrought emotions describe my affect, and I'm vehemently telling myself not to do anything without calculation. I hand Ms. Johanon, a psychiatric nurse practitioner, my journal.

"Dr. Tyre and I've been on the phone all morning discussing you," she begins, "and I'll make sure that Dr. Tyre's supervisor reads your journal," she pauses. Then Ms. Johanon continues, "Dr. Tyre and her supervisor have agreed to meet with you next Monday. Is that all right?"

A weak nod affirms my reluctant agreement to the only presented option. The session is a "carbon copy" of last evening's emergency room session. I explain in detail about my chaotic therapy with Dr. Tyre. Ms. Johanon seems uninterested and eventually redirects the conversation to finding out if I'm suicidal....

All of a sudden she asks, "Are you thinking of hurting Dr. Tyre?"

"Why no!" I quickly answer. Shortly after that, she excuses herself.

Beth says, "I don't understand why she's asked you about hurting Dr. Tyre. Maybe, Dr. Tyre has been telling her crazy things about you." Ms. Johanon returns twenty minutes later and asks if I want daily clinic appointments.

"Yes," I respond. The session ends.

New Record: Crisis and Brief Therapy Service 10/24

C&BTS One and one half hour 10/24 S/O "I've been in

regression x 2 days, I'm so depressed I think about killing myself."
Pt. was also seen last eve in E.D. He was seen today with his wife,
Beth. He talks about a possible conspiracy here at UHMC, talks
quietly, appears somewhat paranoid. Expresses anger at
psychiatrist Dr. Tyre, saying she is mean, vindictive and nasty and
that "she is going to do me in at the end." Pt. is negative homicidal
ideation, some suicidal ideation, but able to contract for safety and
see me in the AM. He wanted his appointment on Thursday with
Dr. Tyre canceled and the plan was for him to be seen on Monday
10/30 at 1:00 PM with Dr. Tyre and Dr. Miller, her sup. Trudy J.
Johnan, ARNP. Received phone call from Mr. Lynch who has
talked with Dr. Tyre. He plans to see her Thurs. He states he feels
much better.

By Tuesday afternoon "things," as one might say, have
emotionally calmed down, so I telephone Dr. Miller to make
sure he will read my journal—It's critical! He is short and curt
with me and says, "I have no intention of reading your journal
and if I did you'd have to pay me to do it!" The angry tone in
his voice startles me. I know I ought to say something to
encourage him to read my journal, but at this moment in my
weakened state it seems impossible.

"I've a lot of problems in therapy. Can I, at least, bring my
journal with me?" I meekly ask.

"That will be all right," he replies; then he adds, "We're
only going to meet for fifty minutes."

When I hang up I feel quite a surge of guilt because he
seems mad at me, too. No one cares about the quality of my
therapy; it's surreal to me.

All my streets are dead ends, so I call Grace at home and
say, "I'm sorry for the way I've acted in therapy and for going
to the emergency room."

"Your apology is accepted," she answers pleasantly. Then,
I call Dr. Barber and Ms. Johanon and tell them that Dr.
Miller has refused to read my notes. My hope is that Ms.
Johanon or Dr. Barber will suggest another avenue but neither
does.

Despite reservations, I expect good to come from Dr.

Miller's meeting, still, however, there's Grace to deal with on Thursday. By now her erratic behavior has become alarming, and all I know right here is that I'm not going to fall deeper and deeper into crazy behaviors with her—no more *therapy* for me. And here's how: no talking about my personal feelings, absolutely no behaviors that can be construed as confrontational, and no sexual discussions. When the session arrives, I am quiet; my inner self feels strong and directive. Go and figure things out, keep your mouth shut, don't do anything in a hurry, and stay out of trouble, I firmly order myself.

Session 10/26

As the session opens Grace hurriedly says, "I want you to know how much I care for you. I spent much of Tuesday morning talking with Trudy Johanon about you, and it was my idea to arrange the meeting with Dr. Miller so you could get your staff consultation. You'll meet with both of us Monday. I'll be there, too."

"OK," I reply in a shallow voice. Nevertheless, my idea is different—an independent psychiatric evaluation without her.

"How are you doing?" asks Grace. "Do you want to discuss Monday's session?"

"No."

"Are you mad at me?"

"No."

"What have you been doing?"

"Nothing."

"I want you to understand you haven't done anything wrong in here. Your swearing and saying f— is completely appropriate." It sounds, *vaguely*, like something she has said before.

"Maybe," I reflect to myself, "by your standards but not by mine." Grace continues to question me similarly and I answer with one or two words....

After fifteen minutes she begins staring at me. I know she wants me to look away, but I won't do it: I pray, bite my tongue, and think abstractly to hold my stare.... Ten, maybe, fifteen minutes pass. Finally she stops staring and starts making "funny faces at me," the kind an adult makes to force a child to respond: her lips become contorted, her eyes widen, and her cheeks puff out. Then in a flash she makes a different contorted face, and another, and another,... When I don't respond, she stops.

After forty–five minutes of vainly trying to engage me in dialogue, her affect shows frustration and annoyance. In a way, I'm doing the staring therapy, and she's today's patient. From nowhere comes the question, "Have you thought about killing yourself?"

"Sure, I had OCD," I reply quickly in a neutral tone.

"Do you have a gun?"

"Yes."

"Why don't you give your gun to a friend to hold?"

What a scenario she presents: I visit a friend and say, "Would you mind holding my gun for a few days...?" Why doesn't my therapist suggest that I give the gun to her or her representative? Too much responsibility?

"Even if I throw my gun down a well," my voice is low, "I can think of a hundred ways to kill myself. So why bother a friend?"

"Why would you want to throw your gun down a well?" Grace asks seriously, pauses, watches for my reaction, and continues, "How would you kill yourself if you didn't use a gun?"

"It would be easy," I begin, remembering what an anesthesiologist friend said in a light literary discussion, "I'd...."

"Why haven't you killed yourself?"

"My love for Beth and my faith in God," I respond.

"I want you to know I care for you like Phil, my son. I couldn't stand anything happening to you. You're an important part of my...."

If you were so concerned about me, I conclude, why did you send me to the ER? You would have come to the hospital for Phil. Without doubt, her words ring empty, hollow, and untrue in my mind.

At the very end of the session Grace asks, "Are you sure you still want to meet with Dr. Miller this Monday? Perhaps, you've changed your mind?"

"No, I haven't." The session is over, and I leave. As I walk down the corridor, I'm feeling vaguely ashamed for being so outwardly placid but inwardly strong and on fire.

Session 10/26 One and one–half hour psychotherapy Ativan 0.5 mg QD PRN

Pt. called after last session + requested emergency #'s again; did in fact come in to ED + to crisis service the following day. Expressed anger re: therapy, fear that it was not being done well, fear that he was functioning less well. No suicidal ideation on Monday night, but pt reportedly express active suicidal ideation the next day (he now denies any active suicidal ideation, saying the interviewer asked leading questions + jumped to conclusions.) Pt. ultimately called me, apologized + confirmed our meeting for today. Pt. was discussed with Dr. Miller x 3 on Tuesday. Today, pt. was nearly silent, answering questions in monosyllabic monotone, until the question of suicidal ideation was explored in detail.

Pt. states he plans to attend a concert with wife tonight, has no increased OCD symptoms; stated he planned to "do what I'm told" by therapist. When this was interpreted as child–like, expressing a sense of abandonment by pulling back from therapist, and a sense of having done wrong, feeling guilty, he seemed momentarily to acknowledge that might be so. Re: suicidal ideation, he initially said "I do not know" whether he'd be safe (in a few different forms); when emphatically told that I need to know he is safe, that he is valuable + his death would not be okay, that I need credible reassurance, he relaxed + explained his spiritual beliefs would prevent him from suicide action, and that he'd go to wife if he did have suicidal ideation. No homicidal ideation or suicidal ideation, pt. is credible. I believe safe. We will meet with Dr. Miller Monday, with goal of shifting to slightly less intense therapy model.

Needing professional advice, I telephone my retired, prior psychiatrist, Dr. Ramos. It is distressing to learn he is ill and dying. "John," he emphatically says after I describe the situation, "terminate her services. Relationships like this are destructive. Keep pushing until you get a senior staff consultation." Then he advises, "Get another psychiatrist to take you out of transference with her."

I trust his judgment implicitly; nevertheless, I find myself paralyzed between transference love for Grace and leaving therapy. Patience is called for. Cautiously voice your therapeutic concerns and try to get on equal footing with them, I command myself.

Session 10/30

Dr. Miller is sitting on the couch when I enter Grace's office. He's fortyish and has a beard. "Do you want me to explain how this meeting came about?" asks Grace after we sit.

"No," I reply. "I know exactly how this meeting was arranged.... Remember, I agreed to it last session."

Dr. Miller says, "I'm solely here as an observer. Dr. Tyre will conduct the session, so you're to talk with her not me." There's a prolonged silence. He looks at me and I at him. Grace remains still and wordless. The silence in the room becomes louder... louder... louder.

Dr. Miller's words rush forth, "What are your concerns Dr. Lynch?"

"Therapy's chaotic and there's a lot of...."

"You know," he rudely interrupts, "that Dr. Tyre is an inexperienced resident. And you knew it when she selected you as her patient!" Sounding annoyed and angry, he reminds me of a high school principal admonishing a student for disruptive behavior.

"Sure I did," I reply nonconfrontationally, "but in one session Grace left the computer flashing and buzzing even though I asked her to turn it off." Her inexperience is no excuse for this error, and we all know it.

"Dr. Tyre runs therapy anyway she wants!" harshly he retorts, his tone cutting. A mixture of common sense, coupled with a certain half naive conception of the common weal, tells me nothing I say to him will count. Grace remains sphinx like, never speaking as I continue through a litany of therapy complaints: numerous uncalled for interruptions, Grace's mercurial behaviors, not calling me a name....

"Dr. Tyre sets the rules and you're to follow them," he answers time and time again, like a power charged drill sergeant.

"But," I reply, "there are no rules except for touching and limited swearing...."

Interrupting aggressively, his tone screeching in authority, "Dr. Tyre sets the rules!"

"Can't someone read my journal?" I ask at this point.

"No, it won't be read. Dr. Tyre is a well supervised resident. In fact, I ordered her to stop reading it."

As our dialogue continues he often interrupts me, quipping at one point, "Perhaps you need a different kind of therapy. This kind of therapy may not be right for you.... Perhaps, you need a different therapist." Intimidated, unsure, I remain silent although what I need to ask is how to get out of transference to find that new therapist.

"Your problem," his look shrewd, determined, "is that you don't know how to properly complain about therapy and express aggression." Interesting conclusion he has made. I have spent week after week voicing my concerns, but I don't contradict him. Obviously, he is defensive and strongly guarding her, but why? And why isn't she defending her own therapy? The session unfolds like this until I comment, "If Grace would have talked with me on the phone, I wouldn't have gone to the ER."

Here she speaks finally and remarks, "I told him to take a walk, eat dinner and take a pill," her voice, timid, unsure. Then she asks me, "What did you want me to say to you?" Her comment startles Dr. Miller and me. After all, who is the therapist and who is the patient!

I know what I wanted her to say— it's all common sense, "You're in trouble so please call me later tonight if you need me. I'll meet you in the ER if you must go." And most importantly, "Our relationship is still strong and solid, and

I'm going to be there for you as promised."

"Therapy's not done on the phone!" Dr. Miller bellows out before I can respond.

"What are all those emergency crisis numbers doing in the phonebook," I speechlessly conclude, "if not to conduct therapy at an emergency level?"

Grace looks so lost that I go to her aid, "Dr. Tyre didn't have time to get to know me as a person," I say; then I add, "I went into transference after a few sessions...."

He interrupts, his voice loud, sharp,"You don't have to make excuses for your therapist!" Here, I comment that my previous therapist has said therapeutic relationships like ours are harmful. Glaring, disdaining eyes offer up his wordless response.

Looking at Grace he asserts, "Dr. Tyre might want to decrease your sessions to one each week." When she doesn't answer, he repeats his statement...then again....

She eventually replies, her voice low, "The last time I did that he went into a stronger transference." Dr. Miller repeats his suggestion; still, Grace doesn't agree.

Finally, Dr. Miller gives her a direct order, "Dr. Tyre will meet with you only once each week."

"But why are you reducing my sessions?" I ask. "Isn't therapy supposed to support me in stressful times?" He doesn't answer. Next, I express my concern about Grace canceling sessions. He waits for her to respond; she doesn't.

After a long hesitation, he gives her another direct order by saying, "Dr. Tyre will meet with you every week. She'll reschedule appointments if she cancels." Still, Grace remains wordless. Finally, after an hour and ten minutes, he stands up to leave seeming very annoyed at Dr. Tyre. He doesn't speak to or look at her, shakes my hand, and says, "Dr. Lynch, you're a smart guy, and you'll figure it all out." Walking down the hall, I realize I've got to leave her. I'll force myself to go to Florida, maybe, distance will do it.

Session 10/30 One hour psychotherapy
Met with pt. & Dr. Miller. Reviewed events of the last week. Pt. explained that he has found regression helpful to him, and that he finds it difficult to restrict his verbalizations when regressed. Dr. Miller reviewed boundaries, emphasizing the need to maintain super ego functioning during sessions, **(Following was added on later note)** and safety between sessions if possible; if not possible, then dynamic psychotherapy may not be appropriate therapy modality. Pt. also described calling me after therapy last week & feeling he was not helped—I suggested eat supper, a walk, Ativan & f/u **(Follow–up)** in our next therapy session, which seemed inadequate to him. Unable to state what he needed when he called during today's session **(The preceding "call" is an error.)**
    O: Pt. was partially unshaven but otherwise (well) appropriately dressed. Affect constricted, often angry. TP logical & coherent. TC negative suicidal ideation negative, homicidal ideation negative psychosis. A/P Although pt. states regression is useful—and this week is minimizing the distress, inc. SI, of last week—I am concerned that B/W **(Bi–Weekly)** therapy is posing overwhelmingly intense currently. Dr. Miller concurs strongly. Based on pt's affect, I do not think he is in agreement with our assessment, or that at present he follows our reasoning as to why frequency of sessions should be decreased. I will explore this further with him—he currently denies feeling rejected, but this may be what is happening. RTC 1 week. **(No Supervisor note)**

    Tuesday I phone Dr. Tyre, "This is Dr. Lynch," I say cordially and add, "I'm leaving for Florida in four weeks and would like to be taken out of transference."
    "Fine," she answers. "I'll start taking you out next session."
    "You know," I continue, "we didn't have a regular session this week."
    "That's your fault!" she rebuts in an abrupt tone. "You're the one who asked for the meeting with Dr. Miller...!" She hasn't been nice about it. The conversation ends.
Session 11/06
    Dr. Tyre arrives ten minutes late although I am her first appointment. After I'm seated, she crosses her legs and pulls

her dress up entirely exposing her cowgirl boots. Her outward appearance confuses and angers me. She is resplendent in her long dark print dress and sienna cowgirl boots. She hasn't worn them since the "mental sex" with me session and their sexual representation is obvious: What is her motive? Why now when I want to leave transference? Why now, when there is so much emotional distress in my life? Experience tells me to proceed very cautiously and find out what she is up to. This cautiousness drives me as I make the "V" peace sign.

"There'll be none of that in here!!" a screaming Dr. Tyre explodes jumping up in her chair. Exploding again, "There'll be none of that in here!!!"

"None of what?" startled, I reply and ask her, my voice steady, "Am I not allowed to make the peace sign in therapy?"

"Oh, that's what it was," she remarks more to herself than me.

"Yes, it was used as a peace symbol during the Vietnam War Era, and it's also how Boy Scouts hold their fingers when they recite their oath."

"You're here to make peace today?"

"Absolutely!" I reply while thinking, "No more craziness in therapy by my doing, no matter what!!"

"I want you to know that I haven't been the perfect mother for you," says a recomposed Grace. "But I've been a good mother. Remember when I gave you five tranquilizers?"

With a head nod, I respond affirmatively.

"Well," she proceeds, "that was a sign to show you how much I cared for you."

"That was very thoughtful of you. Thanks for being such a good mother," I reply nodding again.

"Don't you think," she suggests, "that some women shouldn't be mothers," pausing, watching for my reaction, "like your real mother?"

I nod with mock approval.

"And remember, you don't have to be the perfect son either with me."

"That's nice to hear because I'm far from perfect."

Grace casts a brilliant smile; then pauses as it settles onto me before she continues, "At Christmas time I'm going on vacation. I'll make sure you're prepared for my absence."

"I've already told you that I'll be going to Florida by this time. Shouldn't I be out of transference?"

A coy smile appears accentuating her lips. She seems suddenly very relaxed. "I'll get you ready, anyway, for my absence." Her words leave me wondering if she thinks she possesses mystical power over me. I silently sit reflecting on that smile, not sure what this new information means except to forewarn me that something is amiss.

We dialogue about my dramatic OCD progress. "Did you know your obsessive personality is used as a coping mechanism? That's good," Grace comments. "You should keep using it this way."

"I will," I reply.

On the surface our conversation is nonconfrontational, but every now and then Grace's tone is barbed. After my swearing, emergency room visit, emergency clinic visit, and meeting with Dr. Miller, she might be very mad at me. Nevertheless, no matter how irritably she acts, I am not stepping out of line! With all that has happened by now, I've lost my remaining trust in her, and I suspect she is up to no good. And, then, Trudy Johanon's words surge forth, "Are you thinking of hurting Dr. Tyre?"

So, I decide to cautiously probe and say, "I've been reading up on transference and have a few questions."

"What can I tell you?"

"I've been reading about patients who had a transference psychosis. What happens to them?"

"We had a lecture on transference psychosis a few months ago, but I didn't think it was important so I didn't pay attention." She measures my affect through narrowed eyes, but not by a movement of my smallest muscle do I respond.

Next I say, "I read about a Borderline Personality Disorder, BPD, in transference last week. Can you tell me something about BPD?"

She slides into thought for the briefest moment; then Grace grabs the Diagnostic and Statistical Manual, DSM IV, from her bookshelf, opens it to the borderline personality disorder section and hands it to me.

"Here," she replies, "this book will describe Borderline Personality Disorder, BPD."

I quickly glance over the nine BPD criteria and place the book down.

"You don't think you're one but you are!" she quickly snaps, her voice authoritative, keenly measuring my reaction. Then she proceeds, "You meet eight out of nine criteria, the only one you don't meet is suicide." She rises and tells me the session is over. I shut down; my hands are cold and clammy as I leave. Walking down the corridor this thought fixes in my mind—Am I her scapegoat? the immediate villain? the person who is to absorb all her malice?

Session 11/6 One hour psychotherapy

Pt arrived today & literally made a peace sign with his hand. Discussed his sense of having progressed far(?), his fascination with transference & regression, his satisfaction that now was good time to stop that kind of therapy; also commented on how much he thought Dr. Miller was like him before he got sick. Is continuing exposures—attending a concert tonight. Functioning & feeling well again.

At this point, his obsessions with contamination are his most troublesome symptom and really has only v. few compulsions, which do not limit social functioning. Affect full, relaxed, friendly with no hostility, no incongruent humor. negative suicidal ideation; negative homicidal ideation.

A/P—Again appears stable, in good control of affect, and with a sense of increased competence. I will explore further his ID with Dr. Miller. Also will start to explore occupational functioning—? volunteer work; and will explore obsessions further. Continue 1 x week, supportive/behavioral/cognitive therapy.

When I arrive in the lobby and meet Beth, I tell her Dr.

Tyre has just diagnosed me with a Borderline Personality Disorder, BPD.

"What else did she tell you?!" alarmingly Beth asks.

"Not much."

"Did she tell you how she arrived at the diagnosis?!"

"No."

"Did she tell you her treatment plan...?!"

"No. Only that I met eight of the nine criteria."

"John, let's walk over to the hospital library so I can read the DSM," suggests Beth.

We go to the hospital library and read the DSM's very unpleasant BPD criteria. Borderline Personality Disorder: is a *severely dysfunctional* form of personality organization and a very damaging label.

Diagnostic Criteria for 301.83 Borderline Personality Disorder DSM III/IV

A pervasive pattern of instability of interpersonal relationships, self–image, affects, and marked impulsivity beginning by early adulthood and present in a variety of contexts, as indicated by five (or more) of the following:

(1) Frantic efforts to avoid real or imagined abandonment. Impulsive actions such as self–mutilating or suicidal behaviors.

(2) A pattern of unstable and intense interpersonal relationships alternating between extremes of idealization and devaluation.

(3) Identity disturbance: markedly and persistently unstable self–image—sudden and dramatic shifts in self–image, characterized by shifting goals, values, and vocational aspirations. There maybe sudden changes in, sexual identity, values and types of friends. These individuals may show worse performance in unstructured work or school situations.

(4) Impulsivity in at least two areas that are potentially self–damaging (e.g. sex, substance abuse).

(5) Recurrent suicidal behavior, gestures, or threats, or

self–mutilating behavior; e.g. cutting or burning and suicide threats and attempts are very common. Recurrent suicidality is often the reason that these individuals present for help.

(6) Affective instability due to a marked reactivity of mood, periods of anger, panic, or despair and is rarely relieved by periods of well–being or satisfaction.

(7) Chronic feelings of emptiness. Easily bored, they may constantly seek something to do.

(8) Inappropriate intense anger or difficulty controlling anger (e.g. frequent displays of temper, constant anger, recurrent physical fights).

(9) Transient, stress related paranoid ideation or severe dissociative symptoms.

These episodes occur most frequently in response to a real or imagined abandonment. Abbreviated (DSM IV).

This horrible psychological profile creates an ache in my gut. Inside I am feeling a deep, dark worry and so is Beth who fearfully says, "This is a bad diagnosis and could destroy our lives!"

As the day wears on I obsess about the BPD personality label. "Have we ever known anyone who has a Borderline Personality Disorder?" I inquire of Beth.

"Not any of our friends," she answers, "but I believe the second criminal in Helen Prejean's book, *Dead Man Walking*, has many borderline characteristics."

"Maybe, she's trying to BPD me to cover her poor therapy," I suggest in an uneasy minute and, then, comfort myself by asserting to Beth, "There's no evidence of these criteria in my life! How can she think I'm such a horrible person! Previous psychiatric evaluations—all by board certified therapists—have only supported OCD as my diagnosis...." Such reassurance is emotionally needed. But instantly, my mind empties of intellectualization and lapses back into a quagmire of bewilderment.

"Perhaps she said it to disrupt you," Beth suggests, "and hasn't written it in your record. There's been the time delay, cowgirl boots, referring to herself as your mother, and her affect being hot and cold. Maybe she's trying to deepen your transference or...." My nerves have become raw.

There's an endless stream of ideas this week, some good, some appalling, all fluently detailed in my mind, yet flawed by my apparent inability to make distinctions.

Session 11/13

Dr. Tyre is dressed to the hilt today and wears an enticing plaid slit skirt. Her makeup, which she almost never wears, is beautifully applied and her hair is most perfectly styled and uncharacteristically pulled back so her dangling earrings are exposed. I camouflage my response although she hugs my shoulder as we walk together toward her office. After sitting she crosses her legs and her broadly slit skirt opens exposing her red leotards. Drawn by male instinct, I look. My eyes nervously widen as she overtly measures my reaction. Slowly and carefully she adjusts her open skirt, it comes open again.... Madness permeates this setting.

The subtle dialogue begins with a chat about chickens. Dr. Tyre has two chickens and a young rooster as pets, "Here's a mail–order bird catalogue that," passing it to her, "I brought for you. Buy a couple of guinea hens, they're very interesting birds."

She smiles and says in reply, "Thanks."

After a few minutes of light chatting, I, with nerves twitching, redirect our conversation. "Dr. Tyre, last week you said I had a Borderline Personality Disorder. I'm sure you understand that Beth and I have been upset all week about it." I'm watchful, but her reaction is nothing graphic. Yet, her derisive pleasure is sensed. Grace with her M.D. behind her name has the power and structure to protect her.... Nonetheless, there is no turning back for me. "Will you please show me the DSM–BPD section again?" She complies. I glance at the criteria although I remember them all too well. "Would you please tell me how I meet these criteria?"

"Why do you want to know?" She recrosses her legs, her skirt comes open, she rewraps it....

"You've made a serious diagnosis. Please tell me what you are basing it on. If I were diagnosed with Diabetes, the physician would tell me how he concluded that diagnosis."

"Why don't you tell me what you think about my diagnosis?" she condescendingly asks.

"I think you're wrong. My life doesn't reflect any of the criteria, but, still, would you, please, explain your diagnosis."

Smugly she speaks, her tone commanding, "When you tell me I'm wrong, you're arguing. And I'm not going to discuss it with you when you're arguing like this."

"Dr. Tyre I'm sorry," quickly I reply, "if you think I'm arguing, but I just want to know what evidence formed the basis for your diagnosis. Perhaps I'm wrong and need to change my viewpoint." My voice is projecting calm and is settled. Nevertheless, a quivering current of emotion flows through me, profound and unidentifiable.

"Maybe another time I'll tell you," tauntingly she retorts. Once more I am pleading with her, desperately. Here my shoulders slouch and I give up. Revulsion seizes me, disgust, loathing for the whole process. I recognize her indication of power and displeasure, an awesome combination, so I choose my words carefully as we go on.

Occasionally as we chat, Dr. Tyre uses an aggressive tone and taunting words. I speculate that perhaps she is trying to entice me into an incident or.... I cautiously counter her behavior by entering into a long soliloquy about my upcoming travel plans.

"I'm going to have a nice winter," I begin. Then I add, "On my way to Florida, I'll visit with my brother, parents, grandmother, an aunt and uncle, and a good friend. Then we're driving in February to Colorado and spending three weeks with other friends and their children.... In Florida we'll be living with and supporting our pregnant tenant. Her husband is away all week in a military training program...." Dr. Tyre has no interest in my words and makes no comment.

But at a pause says, "You're an extremely talented person," wrapping her skirt which has opened again. "What you need to do is make yourself available to the community."

"Like what?" I inquire.

"You should volunteer to work in the library, maybe tutor kids, or better yet, volunteer your services at an elementary or high school as a substitute teacher."

"Years ago I taught both junior and senior high. I liked junior high better," I reply.

"You should be doing it," encouragingly she suggests.

Her comments are constructive and positive; nonetheless, who would want a BPD person to work in a school, especially with young children? Someone like this isn't an appropriate role model for students, and we both know it. At the end of the session, she disrupts me by quipping, "See, we've had a pleasant collegial conversation today. If you keep being nice to me at some point in the future, I'll explain each of your eight BPD criteria and tell you how you can best improve yourself." An affirmation of authority and power over me—how pathetic and desperate I must seem to her to suggest I am both a BPD and wonderful person and for her to believe that I'd go along with it! It's just her madness, this!

The session has seemed too long, yet suddenly too short, as I say to her, "Please, explain how you arrived at the diagnosis based on these DSM criteria."

Condescendingly, she asserts, "The DSM criteria are only a matter of semantics because we professionals don't pay attention to the words. We know what you are!" I shudder to think that Dr. Tyre may be telling me the secretive truth about psychiatry's inner workings. Then she tries to mediate the diagnosis and continues, "I don't understand why you're so concerned, anyway. You know who you are."

But I'll have none of it. "Dr. Tyre, this is a powerful label to put on me!"

"I don't label people! You're a person who can make a contribution to the community by volunteering at a school or library! You're a wonderful person! I'd never put a label on you!"

But I'll have none of it. "Dr. Tyre, did you write this

diagnosis in my record and if so, when did you do it?"

"Yes. Several weeks ago Dr. Miller made the diagnosis, and now I agree with him."

"But Dr. Tyre, how could Dr. Miller make a diagnosis when he hadn't yet met me?"

There is silence. She has learned quite well that the silent never bear witness against themselves. Silence remains until she says, "Your time's up." Walking out the door I realize that my exploratory sanctuary has become my hell on earth.

Session 11/13 One hour psychotherapy

Pt. discussed upcoming plan to travel and visit friends this winter. OCD symptoms do not appear to be limiting him significantly at this point; in fact, they appear to be functioning as a way to cope with internal chaos and actually maximize functioning. Able to tolerate emergency dental visit. Pt. expressed anger and disbelief re: diagnosis of BPD **(No diagnosis, assessment or plan noted in previous record)** but was easily redirected and reassured re: his good level of functioning. Negative suicidal ideation; negative homicidal ideation; negative psychosis.

A/P Stable Functioning is now dramatically improved and consistently improved compared with initial visit. I have encouraged pt. to begin seeking volunteer work; clearly he is still very fragile, but is now able to do some meaningful work and should do so to maximize functioning.

Beth has to drive me home from therapy. That evening a worrying Beth calls a friend to obtain much needed advice. Her advice is clear: the BPD diagnosis is wrong and damaging. "Cut your losses and leave," she tells Beth. She then goes on, "I've done mental status examinations for twenty years, and John is certainly not a BPD." She suggests to Beth, "Get John's records and see what is written on them."

"How difficult will that be?" Beth asks.

"Usually they resist and offer you only a summary record or a paid reading with the therapist. Even if University refuses to send your records," she continues, "keep pushing because legally they have to give you a copy." Beth and I feel lucky to have this good friend.

Tuesday afternoon I telephone Dr. Tyre and say, "Your services are terminated, and I want you to arrange for a senior consultation."

She responds quickly, "No, you can't terminate me on the telephone. You must come into therapy on Monday." I insist as strongly as my weakened self allows, but she curtly refuses and quips, "Therapy's not done on the phone. Sorry, I have to go. See you on Monday. Goodbye."

CHAPTER 18

By now, I realize that therapeutic models create rifts in one's psyche as they only encourage a negative focus while ignoring the positive healing aspects, such as friendship, empathy, love, and God; so my journal perspective changes. Indeed, reflecting back, I was a lucky child in many ways and was given more than many. God has given me the opportunity to explore my subconscious mind's deepest caverns and to feel the pain. I am more integrated as a person and have grown as a Christian.... I know my feelings better now than at anytime in my life.... My relationship with my parents is reforming and for the better, although it is a slow process.

Later in the week Beth and I discuss the danger of others finding out about this diagnosis. It is the age of extensive computer data banks—from those of health insurance and health maintenance organizations to everything in between: privacy violations are commonplace. We also know that even the privacy rights for psychiatric/AIDS patients are not observed as diligently as people think. For a few years Beth administered a hospital quality assurance program which was responsible for investigating complaints of psychiatric patents whose diagnoses had been breached. She also discovered that unauthorized staff knew the names of the nine HIV infected staff.

As I walk through the hospital, I pray with these words: "God give me the strength to leave her." I know that today, like always, she will be playing a terrible mind game. She always will be, even if we do therapy through eternity. I arrive ten minutes early. I do not know whether I will be attracted or repelled by her, but only that I will be deeply moved at the end.

Session 11/20

At 11:00 A.M. Dr. Tyre sends her secretary, the first time ever, into the reception area to tell me that she is going to see another patient during my time, and I must wait. The secretary leaves with the woman.

After a twenty–minute delay, my session begins as I tell Grace how much Beth and I enjoyed the University Gospel Choir on Saturday and about my OCD progress. Inevitably I say, "Dr. Tyre, you told me last week I've a lot to offer the community and I should volunteer my services with children in a school district. I'm wondering if I can start coaching a junior high girls' or boys' athletic team?"

She replies, "You like kids and I think that would be a good idea, but what would you do about the blood if someone were injured?"

"That's what getting well is about," proudly I answer and, swiftly, proceed, "Beth and I would like to take in a foster child."

"What age group?"

"Six to nine."

"That's a good idea, and I recommend it." As our dialogue continues it's obvious we are in a high level mental mind game.

Abruptly in a rejecting, sarcastic, raised tone, she sharply says, "Don't call me at home anymore unless it's an absolute emergency!!"

"I'm sorry," I quickly apologize taken by surprise, "but the reason was only to terminate you."

"I don't care what the reason is! Don't call me at home!!"

The misdiagnosis is my concern, so I change subjects and remark, "Dr. Tyre, how can a person who has Borderline Personality Disorder work with children in a school district? How can I be a foster parent? What am I to tell the school and state authorities if they question me about my psychiatric diagnosis?"

"Just tell any authority who asks that your only diagnosis is OCD. Forget about your BPD diagnosis," she quickly replies.

Her implication alarms me so I inquire, "Are you sure I shouldn't tell the state authorities about my BPD diagnosis?"

"I'm sure! Don't tell them that I've diagnosed you with BPD. Just tell them you have OCD!" assuredly she avows. Obviously she knows quite well that BPD is an extremely serious diagnosis; otherwise, why not disclose the diagnosis?

Further dialogue only repeats the implicit messages: she is the expert, and I don't know anything about Borderline Personality Disorder. "Why are you making such a big deal about it?" Dr. Tyre interjects at one point. She then says, "There's a...here at University and...that person works in the...and...."

I fall into emotion, my self shrinking into confusion. Finally I say to break another eerie silence, "No one in my life has ever said a more hurtful thing to me."

"I never told you to hurt you!" Grace responds; then she repeats, "Why do you care anyway! You know who you are!" I have resigned myself to "whatever," so I just sit in a painful emotional state, with sweaty palms, emotionally shivering.

The session is ending, so I take a deep breath to find the strongest part of myself and assert, "Grace, you are terminated as my therapist, and I want a senior consultation with Dr. Tom, the head of the residency program." Her face drops in dismay and disbelief.

Immediately she tries to talk me out of my decision. "Why do you want to create trouble for yourself? Your record will show two borderline diagnoses!" She goes on and on, appealing externally, but her widened eyes and glaring look show she is seething internally, "You're still in transference, that's a reason to stay with me...! I'll always be your therapist and you can come back anytime...!"

"Sorry, but I'm leaving and want a copy of my records."

"I can't do that, but you can come in and I'll read them with you."

"I know my legal rights," firmly and authoritatively I reply. Again I ask her to make an appointment with Dr. Tom.

"I'll do it right away, but you're asking for trouble if you appeal a diagnosis in psychiatry! No one will change it!" Her tone is flat.

It is a painful moment when I tell her I will always have love in my heart for her and will pray for her tonight. She refuses to acknowledge my prayer and does not express good will toward me; nevertheless, I reach out and shake her hand goodbye. She looks at me as I take my first step toward the door. She looks at me without having the slightest idea of who I am or what is in my head. She looks as I take another step and I know she doesn't know how to hold me as my hand falls on the doorknob. Then she gives up and turns away. I am deeply moved by today's outcome because I still harbor transference–induced feelings of love toward her and want desperately to see her again. Therapy has been left behind but not my transference.

Session 11/20 One hour psychotherapy/termination

Pt. called last week requesting termination (called me at home); redirected to present this in session today. Initial discussion of plans to explore coaching or short–term foster care as activities which I agree pt. is safe & competent to do & would pull in his defense of altruism. Again questioned diagnosis of BPD, stating that he does not want to be viewed as a substance abuser or "slasher." Description of behaviors in the transference which had led Dr. Miller & then myself to see pt as borderline briefly offered but not acknowledged by pt.

He expressed concern re: the affect of this diagnosis on future employability, but rejected my suggestion that, as his disability is secondary to OCD, he not mention other diagnoses. Finally, pt. stated that he saw this diagnosis as a rejection of him by a maternal figure. I strongly encouraged him to continue therapy long enough to address this feeling of rejection, but pt. stated he would not. Requested 1) eval by Dr. Tom to, if possible R/O BPD; and 2) a copy of confidential records. Again, stated therapy had been v. helpful overall.

O: Good grooming; good eye contact; shook hands at end of session. Affect full, generally congruent, some anger, quite guarded. Negative suicidal ideation. A/P Stable. Termination of therapy was anticipated by Dr. Miller. He is safe & competent to make this decision. I will call re. ? eval by Dr. Tom after speaking with Drs. Tom/or Miller.

D/W **(Discuss with)** Art Brison, Risk Management. **(Legal department)**

That afternoon I send Dr. Tom, the residency director, a letter asking for his immediate assistance. Two anxious weeks pass in which neither he nor Dr. Tyre contact me. Worrying, I call her—after four attempts we speak.

"What's up?" abruptly she asks.

"Have you made my appointment with Dr. Tom?"

"No, I haven't! You can make it yourself!"

"How about my records? You were going to look into that matter, too."

"Ask him about them! I have to go." Her response has been unhelpful, rejecting, and unprofessional.

Dr. Tom says to my call, "I've been too busy to contact you. I'll see you on the sixth at 1:30 P.M.."

Session 12/06

Dr. Tom arrives promptly, introduces himself, and escorts Beth and me to his office. Once seated he asks, "Why are you here?" For certain everyone knows why I'm here. Is he, like Grace, unwillingly to speak directly to an issue? More and more psychiatry seems like a pseudo game of theoryless, coy–innuendos. My records, starkly, sit on his desk.

Experience tells me to begin this way for I've learned not to say too much too soon in psychiatry. "I want to tell you about myself and Beth will do the same." We know that once he hears I did this..., this..., and that..., I'll prove without any doubt I'm not a BPD. We both highlight our individual histories and our life together. He silently listens.

Eventually, recasting subjects when the ground seems safer, I comment, "My therapy was chaotic and confusing."

"Why?" he asks.

"In the last session Grace said that she hadn't been a perfect mother...."

Dr. Tom ignores the comment and asks, "It's my understanding that you had a chaotic relationship with your first therapist?" He seems pleased to be on the offensive.

"Not so," Beth interjects, hands him a letter, and proffers, "here's a letter from that therapist which clearly shows the opposite."

For a moment Dr. Tom's tensile strength appears to be weakened. He hesitates, reads the letter and, then, asks, "What else do you want to tell me?"

"Well, for one thing there weren't boundaries in the therapy..., insufficient monitoring and interpretation of my transference..., and Dr. Tyre has refused to call me by name even after I..., and she agreed to do it."

"I call patients by name," Dr. Tom remarks proudly at this point, and Dr. Tom supports Grace with a justification by saying, "Aren't there people in your life who don't call you by name?"

Two astonished, penetrating stares now confront him. "Sure," I conceptualize, "the highway toll collector...." He stops speaking suddenly, perhaps, realizing how foolish he is sounding by justifying a dehumanization methodology.

Dr. Tom brings up the next matter and looks at me vigilantly, "Dr. Tyre has told me you're in love with her."

"Sure, I had childhood transference love for her."

"But you can't always be certain that it's transference love," he assuredly comments. Obviously, Dr. Tyre has told him, much....

"Beth and I have made interpretations about this love...." At this point I mention my journal that nobody will read.

"Can I see it, Dr. Lynch?" asks Dr. Tom.

"Certainly," I hand it to him while mentioning my OCD progress. After a minute of flipping pages, he hands it back. Neither Beth nor I reflect surprise when he does not ask to read it or about my OCD progress.

"What did you think of Dr. Tyre?" he inquires next.

"Dr. Tyre is an inexperienced therapist who couldn't handle the emotional turmoil of a transference relationship, but from what I know she is a good mother to her children, and I wish she had been my mother."

Cautiously, I now mention the BPD diagnosis and how it

occurred. "Dr. Tom," I begin anxiously with my nerves twitching, "Dr. Tyre handed me the DSM, and she told me I met eight of the nine criteria, and she ended the session without another word. She didn't give me one reason for her diagnosis or propose a treatment plan."

Emphatically, Beth adds, "We're very concerned because BPD is a damaging diagnosis."

"Yes it is," agrees Dr. Tom, "but," he continues, "BPDs can be looked at in many different ways."

He is not going to get away with this I decide and declare, "Isn't that why the DSM was developed because there were so many arbitrary and capricious psychiatric diagnoses?" Dr. Tyre's words rang in my mind: "These criteria are a matter of semantics. We psychiatrists don't pay attention to them."

"BPDs do well in structured environments," he quickly counters, directing us elsewhere. I tell him again that my entire work history and life have always been unstructured: in teaching and in tennis where I was self–directed, creating my own structure, my own lessons, and lectures....

"I want you to know that your BPD diagnosis has been mentioned only 'loosely' in the last three sessions...," he graciously offers up.

"What does 'loosely' mean? It's still a diagnosis isn't it?" challengingly I interject.

"Well!" he hesitates, "yes!" his tone lower.

The session is almost over, so I straightaway ask to see my record or chart. He opens it to the first session after the Dr. Miller session and to the following one. As Beth and I glance at the pages, he hurriedly remarks speaking rapidly, "Sorry our time is up." Still, I've seen BPD written ten or twelve times on one record page and on the other six or eight times.

"Can I read my record with Beth in another room?" I ask.

"No, I can't allow that. Why don't you come in and Dr. Tyre will read them to you?" I don't respond and hand them back.

"Do I meet the BPD criteria?" I ask, standing. My eyes are

fixed on him.

His face droops in dismay. "No, you don't meet the BPD criteria. But there's no way your record can be changed!" he assertively and confidently replies.

Beth aggressively responds, "You mean a hospital record can't be corrected if it's in error?!"

He repeats, "The diagnosis can't be changed in your record. That's correct! But if you like," he cordially suggests, "you can attach a personal note stating you disagree," words of inconsequentiality, for sure.

"I spoke with Dr. Fong, my first therapist, and he has suggested I get an independent evaluation with Dr. Gold, the head of the practice," confidently I say. Dr. Tom's affect turns nervous.

"I don't know whether that's possible," he comes back anxiously. "I don't think it can be done."

"That's what we want and will settle for nothing less," I reply firmly, confidently, with Beth hugging my side.

"I'll arrange it," reluctantly he answers.

12/6 One hour psychotherapy with pt./W (Wife)/Eval.

S/O (Subjective/Objective)

Pt. asked to see me for staff consultation. Initially hard for me to determine what he/W wanted to get out of meeting—he/W started out by telling me about their lives overall, then his last 3 sessions of therapy and his feeling of Dr. Tyre's mishandling things re his ? diagnosis of BPD. He then went on to describe his view of therapy before that, how chaotic it was. General stuff seemed to me to be that he viewed Dr. Tyre as inflexible, withholding, although he also felt he had benefitted much from the therapy. He showed me his (extensive) journal, which described some fairly intense transferential feelings, which he felt were direct displacements from earlier figures, e.g. female friend in Hawaii.

I discussed with pt./W my view of transference, the term "borderline" (incl. that there were multiple ways of looking at this), *(Perhaps, Dr. Tyre's statement that the DSM is only semantics to psychiatrists is accurate)* reassured pt. that BPD appears loosely in chart, that only OCD was submitted to insurance companies, that he could put something in chart, saying he disagreed with diagnosis if he wished (that we could not delete anything from chart). **(Not true)** At end pt. stated that he'd like an independent evaluation by Dr. Gold (recommended by Dr. Fong) without his referring to previous records. I told him I would look into that.

ASS: **(Assessment)** White male with OCD. Not clearly BPD on this interview—definitely had strong transference reaction, demonstrating persistence in protesting perceived misdiagnosis, therapeutic wounds. PLAN: I spoke with Dr. Gold, will write pt. letter. William Tom

Before we have left the hospital I anxiously begin our dialogue. "Dr. Tom's the person in charge of the residents, in charge of their training, and teaching them what is right and wrong; he admits that her diagnosis is wrong and he says no one can change her 'error' in my record...."

"Even if he writes that you're not a BPD on his record, who's to know that he's the residency director and Dr. Tyre isn't? They both sign their records with M.D., and she's the one that's written the details." Beth also mentions that Dr. Tom is supporting Dr. Tyre's comment that I withhold the truth from government authorities about the BPD diagnosis.

"Try doing that in a court of law and see what happens," is my quick reply. Of course, all this deflects our thinking away from the potential harm Dr. Tyre has done to my mind.

The next day we leave for Florida. As I drive a strong current of intense emotion flows through me, profound and unidentifiable. It's a lengthy trip with all the family and friend visits. Except for a few brief interludes of distraction, I can't get her out of my mind even though I owe her nothing. I know she has used me and that she would do it again if given the chance, and she derives gratification in hurting me.... And I know that for the rest of my life she will pop to and fro in my dreams and sneak into my thoughts bringing back what I need most to forget if I can't find closure. Everything had started out fine, reflecting, I pause, uneasy....

Writing a book will bring me closure and help others, I

decide.

For the next several months, my Florida days mirror my Maine days. From 4 A.M. to 6 A.M. I meditate and pray in bed; here God gives me strength. My emotions set the day's writing tone. Those things I want to forget, my therapist, therapy, and childhood, never leave me—every word feels wonderful or horrible, there's nothing in between and seldom an emotional rest.

In February Beth and I visit with our closest friends in Colorado. It has now been ten weeks since I spoke with Dr. Tyre. In Colorado I call her about my records. Grace calls back. We speak briefly about them and, then, chat pleasantly about snowshoeing. At the conversation's end strong feelings pour out and capriciously I say, "Take care of yourself."

She responds, softly, caringly, "And you take care of yourself." Except for my ER visit, I do not think I ever felt more unsettled inside. So unsettled, in fact, that Beth and I return to Florida the next day. Can I not rid myself of her? I must!

In March I return for my appointment with the head of the psychiatric practice, Dr. Gold, who is also a professor and department chairperson at University Medical Center. With many weeks of editing my journal behind me, I know that I have been through one rugged therapeutic experience. My therapist, Dr. Tyre, has done exactly what my mother did. She told me I am a good kid—bad kid: classic double–bind conditioning. Grace has been mostly rejecting, cold, and unforgiving in the process.

To straighten out the twists and tangles in my mind, I need to discuss my therapy with another therapist at University. After which, I could meet with Dr. Tyre and this therapist to find closure. Getting the BPD diagnosis off my record is most important. On the way to meet with Dr. Gold, I reflect on Dr. Tyre's prior words, "Who's making you feel very small and insignificant?" My answer: Psychiatry!

Session 3/27

Beth and I arrive early for our meeting. The secretary

remarks, "Dr. Gold's been waiting for you." Immediately he appears, introduces himself, and escorts us, using the back door to his office. Once seated he says, "I'm only going to meet with you for one time because I'm not taking new patients." As with Dr. Tom, I discuss my life and Beth discusses her's....

When finished he asks, "Why did you come to University for treatment?" his tone, fast, sharp—reflecting the unpleasant innuendo—why us! There's a contagious, buzzing tension in him. On the contrary, my inner knowledge that I am not a BPD calms me.

There's talk of my OCD and other therapies, but when I mention Grace's therapy, he abruptly cuts me off, raising his voice and seeming inwardly annoyed and angry. "Who knows what happened in there?!" he rebuts with considerable force. "Maybe that resident went into transference with you!" Hurriedly he changes topics and asks about our sex life.

"Our sex life is fine," I reply.

"We've had a good sex life for twenty–six years," adds Beth. "We couldn't have children and never adopted because of my career," hesitating with a painful expression.... Beth pauses again as Dr. Gold's expression quickly turns quizzical, more anxious....

Dr. Gold is very skilled at what he does. First he builds up my confidence by saying, "You don't need any therapy. You're not defective as a human being in anyway." He tells me again I am not defective, providing me with his subliminal message, that I am not a BPD.

Eventually, forming my words carefully I say, "Dr. Tyre has diagnosed me as having BPD."

Emphatically, authoritatively, he replies, "You've been married for twenty–seven years! People with BPD aren't married that long! You don't meet any of the criteria! You're not defective...!!" his tone raised. Then he adds, "You were just trying to get well. That's all." *An exact journal line.* Again, I bring up my chaotic therapy with Dr. Tyre. He shrugs me off and counters, "Like I already said, who knows what happened in there? Maybe the resident went into transference with you." By now I've learned not to say too much with psychiatrists, so there's no challenge. Yet, both Beth and I know painfully well what happened "in there," and we deeply hoped he would discuss it.

Here I mention that I visited with my brother when returning from Florida. "You visit with your family?" he interjects appearing surprised.

"Certainly," I reply, noting, "I lived with my cousin and his family for two months when I was in Europe several years ago." Noticeably his hands tighten on the chair as a shadow of discontent crosses his face.

We discuss Dr. Fong, my initial therapist. Dr. Gold tells us he is a nationally know psychodynamic therapist.

Dr. Gold's closing assessment and remarks, "You are a recovering OCD patient and got well on your own. You have absolutely no BPD characteristics."

"Will you send us a copy of John's record?" Beth asks.

"It will be sent out tomorrow," he answers leading us down the hallway and out the back door, watching us until we are well down the corridor.

University Medical Center
Physician: Gold   Date: 3/27

Diagnostic evaluation requested by patient and arranged by Dr. Tom. Patient and wife seen together for approximately one hour. 52 year–old appropriately dressed man with stable marriage x 27 years. Presents excellent history for severe obsessive compulsive disorder of at least 8 years duration involving ritualistic behavior, washing, and major fear of contracting disease from door knobs, strangers, etc, especially AIDS. Until past several months, his symptoms severely limited his travel and usual social interaction. In the past has had a trial of Anafranil, psychotherapy, and possibly behavioral therapy(?). Recently, however, has begun to improve on his own and is now able to travel and visit friends.

Mental status is devoid of any major psychiatric diagnosis. He is oriented, cognitively intact, and denies hallucinations & delusions. Maintains an optimistic outlook as OCD recedes.

Diagnosis: 1. OCD severe by history; currently improving.
            2. NO evidence for Borderline Personality Disorder.
Plan: No further psychiatric contact needed.

                                                    Gold

Almost before it began, my therapy moment was over. It had left a haunting and unsatisfied curiosity behind. But after learning of Dr. Gold's unwillingness to discuss in detail my therapy with Dr. Tyre, I had resigned myself not to sow any more seeds: for I knew my only crop would be grief. I had not been hoodwinked or deceived. Determined, committed, and not deceived, I continued to write my book.

CHAPTER 19

My OCD progress has been remarkable, especially since my therapy ended chaotically, confusingly, and distressingly. Progress shows everywhere; for instance, after I terminated therapy Beth had minor out–patient surgery. What an OCD accomplishment it was to walk by myself through a hallway littered with blood–soaked gauze containers, sit with Beth in an out–patient operating room, and purchase a snack for us to eat while she was recovering.

Within my OCD progress, unfortunately, therapy's legacy with Dr. Tyre continued. In March, I read my psychiatric records knowing that painful feelings would come up as I looked through her descriptions of me. Hurt and guilt were felt in about equal parts. When the hurt subsided, troubling thoughts arose. These were not the same records I had read in Dr. Tom's office. Those records had mentioned BPD numerous times. In the current records she noted, "patient complained about his BPD diagnosis," but there's no prior mention of BPD. Tampering with records, legal documents, is a serious matter. But a mixture of common sense and justifiable cynicism told me that proving this would be difficult; Why? The *psychiatric department* has absolute control over their patients' records, not hospital medical records. Even so, I was not content to leave things this way, so I sent a letter to University Medical Center Records Department inferring altered records. The reply from the psychiatric department, ***thirty–five new records***. See below a sample of my new set of records from **Tyre, Johanon, Tom—***Complete records:*

10/16 Tyre 1° Ativan 0.5 1mg.prn. RTC 3 days.(Tyre)
10/24 1 ½ hr psycho-support in C&BTS. (Johanon)
12/6 1 ¼ hr psych/eval. (Tom)

After receiving them I wallowed deep in the darkness of delusion. How bad was my therapy and what had it done to my mind? No one gave me a reason why they were changed....

In late May my life took an unexpected turn. It started when Beth suggested we move to the university area so she could resume her professional life and she hoped I would do the same. My thoughts about the move went from fear to reluctancy; from there, it was a quick journey to agreement and expectation for a new life. After all, there's a certain excitement in change, especially when viewed as a positive life force.

I knew that Dr. Tyre lived in the area and seeing her on occasion with her family, I thought, would eliminate the residue of post–therapy, transference feelings. I was out of therapy and reality seemed different. To again be a productive and responsible community member was keenly important. Hopefully, she would recognize this if we met.

In early June, Beth and I looked at houses around the university area, eventually buying one. Our new home had a lovely solarium where I could write and a spacious kitchen in which Beth could cook. We met with the local Baptist pastor, Reverend Hendrick, to reestablish our ties with the church. Amazingly, he was to be our next–door neighbor, another good sign for my travel back into an OCD–free life. How lucky we were to find the "perfect neighbors."

On July fifth our pastor, also my neighbor, brought his wife and three children to our home. Not long after the introductions were completed, his wife and children talked with Beth as I talked with him. After they left Beth said, "John!" her words rapid, her look disrupted. "Guess who the Hendrick's best friends are? And they've been their best friends for five or six years, too." Before I could respond Beth continued, her words still racing out, "Grace and her family!"

"Wow!" I replied. "The odds of something like this happening must be one in a billion...or more!" my nerves raw. We talked for a while about the whys and wherefores, but they were sheerly nervous remarks. Then I said, "It's improbable that a minister's family and atheist's family would have a long protracted friendship like Alice had described...."

"Alice told me they won't go to church with them," Beth responded. "But there's more!" Beth added, "Did you notice how Sara their 4 year old daughter was afraid of Blarney?" (Laurie our pervious dog had died).

"Yes, I noticed it."

"Well, Alice and her oldest son told me how Grace has a rooster living in her house and that it constantly attacks the kids."

"She has a what, living in her house!?" I responded, shaking my head, wordless. What else was there to do?

"A rooster, like I said," Beth repeated, then went on, "One day Sara came home with band aids all over her legs after Grace had babysat her. They told me the rooster kept attacking her...."

"She lets a rooster run around inside her house and attack kids?" I remarked, my level of concern for these kids rising.

"David told me they would find it by the trail of manure," amazed, at a lost for words, I thought of nothing better than to repeat Beth's words. "Manure in their house. A rooster in the house. They're best friends."

"That's right! That's what the Hendricks told me." Beth assertively replied.

"But why?" I asked in confusion. "Everyone in this farming community knows roosters are mean."

"She's trying to take the aggression out of it. Make it tame!" For a brief moment I thought of my therapy. It was a painful flashback to her..., and my inability to recognize it.

"Let's try to help Sara, so she's not afraid of Blarney!" I suggested. Beth quickly agreed.

That evening Beth and I talked for hours. We came up with an endless stream of ideas about what had happened and why, all flawed, nevertheless, by our inability to tell the difference between them....

For several weeks the Pastor's children lived at our house. We took them everywhere, for ice cream, ... The two oldest boys talked endlessly about the Tyres. Beth and I never said anything about knowing Grace.

In a way the Hendrick boys and I were doing the same thing, trying to figure out the puzzling behavior of the Tyres. By mid–July, Alice and her children had told me about Grace's whole past. They described her mostly in positive ways. Yet my therapy experience had shown me she was an angry and hostile person who savored revenge under a pleasant, controlling affect, and she had the power and influence of psychiatry to protect her.

Still, my focus was primarily on OCD progress, so I walked around the semi–rural neighborhood for three hours every day. The purpose? To meet my neighbors. I was successful and met a group of interesting people. My new OCD freedom gave Beth a chance to resume her career, so she volunteered her professional services at a VA Hospital. She now does volunteer work at the VA several days a week.

During therapy Dr. Tyre had suggested I volunteer my talents at a local school, noting this in the original set of records. It was good advice that I did not forget, so in July I met with the Academy's Head Master, Jane Price. I told her of my experience as a high school and middle school teacher, administrator, and baseball, tennis, and basketball coach. Jane was delighted to have someone with my experience and training be a free volunteer at the Academy. She suggested I volunteer my services for creative writing, coaching, and helping her in administrative/research community matters. Our meeting lasted two hours and was very productive.

In August I played in the UCTEXC benefit tennis tournament. I enjoyed seeing my tennis skills were still there—unexpectedly, I finished second. My prize was an attractive jacket. Nevertheless, my cherished prize was not obsessing when I noticed a band–aid on the court as I was playing.

My OCD improvement was remarkable and stable, quite a contrast to the community relationship I was forming with Dr. Tyre and her family. I have cautioned myself not to say too much here as I know fair people make fair judgements, so here is the correspondence:

The community situation concerned me so much I wrote a letter to Dr. Tyre:

August 12

Dear Grace Tyre:

I am writing you a personal letter because I feel unsettled about our community relationship. I understand what is happening with you and I may understand what is happening with your husband. However, the scope of our interpersonal community dynamics goes beyond the four of us. It includes children and other adults. Here I reference the Hendricks and their children as well as your children and other children in the area.

I had an opportunity to play with Phil, David, and Natalie at the church picnic. There's a lot of kid in me and I relate well to this age group. For several years I worked with problem kids of this age in a school district. Also, I spent many productive years working with kids of this age in athletics. In addition, Phil and David came over to my house and I played Balderdash with them. Phil is sensitive and intelligent. A nice boy. You should be very proud of him.

The three Hendrick children think a lot of you and your husband. David and I have become good friends and he visits me often as do Jonathan and Sara. I do not want my friendship with David to interfere with his friendship with Phil. I am very experienced in such matters, as one might say, and will encourage David in the right direction. He's a good kid, without doubt, and probably won't need any guidance from me. This is good.

As you know I will be working as a volunteer at the Kennite Academy. I met with Jane Price for several hours the other day. My role at the Academy will be coaching, creative writing, and acting as a part day substitute teacher, and perhaps, helping Jane in administrative and community matters. I shall be working mostly with the 7th and 8th graders. I spoke recently with a longtime friend who had been the

Deputy Superintendent of Schools for the State of Pennsylvania. He and I both agreed this is a good age group for me. They are half adult, half child, and need an adult role model who isn't a parent or a teacher. One who is part kid at heart. The model I present to David and his friends. Jane also agreed with me about my role modeling.

Obviously I will be running into Phil, and perhaps your other two boys in one way or another. Please be absolutely assured that Beth and I will treat them the same way that we treat David, Jonathan, and Sara. In fact, the same way we treat all children.

I understand your anger and aggression toward me. Dr. Gold told me you were possibly in transference with me. I have worked myself through most of my transference, but not all. I have learned of the wonderful healing power of transference. What a marvelous benefit it provides when one learns how to harness its energy and direct this energy to productive personality readjustments. However, if a person fails to harness its productive energy and work through their feelings in a positive way, then, I know its healing energy will be wasted.

I realize all the negativity you show toward Beth and me is mostly not about us, although superficially I suspect you are angry because of my case. You may deny this next thought but in my mind when I terminated my therapy, I was thinking of you also. We had created a sort of therapeutic madness whether we like to admit it or not. Since then, I have come far because even though you act so rejecting toward me, it doesn't seem to overly bother me. In fact I sometimes wish you would be even more rejecting so you could work through more intense feelings.

I believe we should talk. That is all four of us or just you and I, it doesn't matter. But you should do most of the talking. If you're angry at me then tell me. I don't mind nor does Beth. I had the opportunity to deal with my feelings through you and you have the opportunity to deal with your feelings through me. You should avail yourself of this unique opportunity. Look where I began and where I am today. An almost completely changed life. All this isn't about, professionalism, training, etc., it's about life and life is our best therapy.

If you want to know anything about me just ask David or Jonathan. Most kids know adults better than most adults. There are other issues that need to be addressed but except for a few final thoughts I wish to go no further. Once again my primary reason for writing is to explain that I understand you and your husband's anger and that Beth and I will treat your children with the same thoughtfulness and caring that we do all children. No matter how you respond I will wave and say hello to you and your husband in a neighborly manner.

We have met a lot of nice people who live on Old Oak Road. Fini is a most interesting person to talk with. She wants to read the finished portion of my Romance Novel, at 82 nevertheless, and gave me a book she wrote about her life in Koln from 1920 to 1944. Marilyn and I talked of going snow-shoeing this winter and we both like sheep and goats. Rebecca and her husband told me to walk all the trails on their property. Your garden is lovely and something to be proud of. Obviously you put a lot of work into it. Fini told me it was beautiful in the spring. It sure is an interesting road to live on.

Today I played in the UTEX benefit tennis tournament and met another interesting person, Anne Marie Robertson, a Fairfield resident a few years back, who wants to play tennis with me. Her husband is a Professor of Chemistry at University. I tell you these things to once again reference the power of transference healing. After all, just over 1 year ago you had to open the door so I could leave the hospital.

John Ivy Lynch

Dr. Tyre didn't answer my letter.

Establishing my life in the community:

In early August the Academy's Headmaster, Jane Price, wrote a letter asking me to contact, Don Potter, the athletic director for a volunteer position.

August 15

Dear John,

It was a pleasure to talk with you earlier this week, and I look forward to more! I'm writing to alert you to a newly opened coaching position here, for Junior Girl's Soccer. Our A.D. Don Potter, would be glad to hear from you if you're interested. He'll be setting up interviews ASAP.

Cheers—Jane

After the August 15ᵗʰ letter Jane Price and Don Potter would not to speak with me:

Don Potter didn't return 5 or 6 calls. Later I called Jane, as she had earlier requested. I called her 4 or 5 times. Jane didn't return my calls. I wrote her a letter. She didn't answer it.

My letter to the head of the psychiatric practice explaining my concern about the community situation:

September 3

Dear Dr. Gold:

It is unfortunate that I must write this lengthy letter but the seriousness of this matter warrants it....

....Then it happened. Towards the end of August, I heard my dog continuously barking and went outside to look around my backyard. There I saw my neighbor, Jonathan, and his friend Allen (Dr. T's second boy) playing. When Allen saw me he appeared frightened and ran and hid behind some logs although Jonathan continued to play. It was the first time in my fifty years that a small child ran and hid at my sight. Of course, I had my suspicion but I realized suspicions don't prove anything, yet, there appeared to be enough evidence to call my neighbors in and find out if Dr. Tyre had violated my right to confidentiality.

....I asked my neighbors to come over. They did. I asked them if the Tyres had mentioned me. They said, yes. I asked them how. Alice responded Don Tyre told them that I was a psychiatric patient of his wife, confidentially, and that his children were not allowed to have contact with Beth or me. Later, because they began to worry about their own children, they spoke directly with Dr. Tyre who told them to keep her children away from Beth and me.

Dr. Lynch

Dr. Gold's reply expressing his concern:

6 September

Dear Dr. Lynch:

I received your September 3rd letter. Obviously, any concern about confidentiality is of concern to us. We will investigate the situation and respond to you in a timely manner.

Adolph Gold, MD

I responded with another letter to Dr. Gold:

October 2

Dear Dr. Gold:

Last week an attorney, Matt Wilson, who represents Anderson International Group called to make an appointment with me. He said he had been assigned Dr. Grace Tyre's malpractice case at your request, and he handled these cases often. I was disheartened to learn that breaches of confidentiality were more common than a person, such as myself, might expect. I wondered, as he spoke, why you had initiated a malpractice case against Dr. Tyre?

My letter of September 3, 1996 asked for an administrative determination of Dr. Tyre's professional conduct. Your reply to this letter suggested an administrative resolution and in no way implied this was a malpractice matter for Dr. Tyre; I remain confused.

There are several issues in my case which I now want to discuss. These issues represent my inquiry into my level of care. In our March 1996 meeting you avoided discussing my level of care concerns, so I wrote you a letter in April 1996 asking for this help. You thought that my suggestion was inappropriate. I reference your April 1996 letter which clearly stated that you would not discuss any level of care issues with me nor would any of your staff at any time.

John Ivy Lynch

Dr. Tyre then hired an attorney even though no action had been taken against her, which I thought breached my confidentiality. This letter was sent to me.

October 10

Dear Mr. Lynch:

I represent Dr. Grace Tyre, her husband, Don, and her family. Dr. Tyre has shared with me your "personal letter" to her dated 8/12/96. I would point out to you that the envelope in which this personal letter came was addressed "Ms. Grace Tyre" to her post office box and bore only a post office box return. It was not addressed to her as Dr. Tyre, nor was it addressed to her at her place of employment where confidentiality regarding its content could be expected. In fact, the letter was actually opened by Dr. Tyre's husband, which is a standard operating procedure in the Tyre household, with the exception of letters addressed to Dr. Tyre with her formal medical title.

Dr. and Mr. Tyre were very concerned about the innuendo of the letter, references to your establishing relationships with their children or them. Your mention in that letter of details regarding your prior physician-patient relationship with Dr. Tyre was indeed unfortunate, inappropriate, and certainly not confidential.

Because of that professional past relationship, it is imperative that you refrain from any social contact with either Dr. Tyre, her husband, or any members of her family and that you refrain from engaging in any encounters, either in the vicinity of the Tyre home or in any public setting.

I have also been made aware that you have made a claim of unprofessional conduct against Dr. Tyre. Dr. Tyre has been advised that matter will be handled by UMC in accord with its usual protocals I wish to advise you that I will likewise render assistance to Dr. Tyre with regard to this allegation. I am sure that you understand that such allegations are taken very seriously by physicians and I would sincerely recommend that you discuss this situation with your own attorney and that you share my letter with that attorney.

It is my opinion that the way in which you have already published information regarding your past treatment history and your claims against Dr. Tyre, has resulted in your making public the information which you claim to have been privileged. I would add that the treatment you received from Dr. Tyre was not only very helpful to you but in keeping with the highest standards of her profession.

Again, let me reiterate that under no circumstances are you to contact or attempt to contact any members of the Tyre family. I am instructing you to refrain from visiting their property. Although I think it is clearly stated above, once again, you are not in any way to contact any of the Tyre children, either directly or indirectly.

David M. Fisher, Attorney

In mid-September I sent a letter to the medical director of the hospital attaching my letter of September 3, to Dr. Gold. This reply arrived before I received the letter from Dr Tyre's lawyer:

October 15

PERSONAL AND CONFIDENTIAL
John I. Lynch, Ed.D.

Dear Mr. Lynch:
I have reviewed your very brief cover letter of October 4,

1996, along with the letter dated October 2, 1996, which you sent to Adolph Gold here at University Medical Center. Having spoken briefly with Dr. Gold, let me first state that it is the opinion of everyone involved with your care at University Medical Center that the treatment and attention that you received was not only of the highest quality but was also extremely beneficial to you. It is clear that as a result of the fine and supportive care which you received you made great strides. All of us at University Medical Center sincerely hope that you are continuing to progress.... Dr. Tyre (and it must be apparent to you that we have the highest regard for Dr. Tyre here at University Medical Center).

Unfortunately, at any time that a patient terminates care and decides to pursue care elsewhere, there is an opportunity for misunderstanding, miscommunication and the like. We at University Medical Center certainly hope that you are continuing successfully with treatment and we certainly encourage you to do so.

Mary L. Myers, M.D.
Medical Director

After receiving the letter from Dr. Tyre's lawyer, I gave the pastor, my neighbor, a copy of it. We had spoken with him about the gravity of this situation for Beth and me in the community on several occasions, but to no avail. Beth and I hoped this lawyer's letter...:

October 18

Dear Pastor Hendrick:

We received this intimidating letter from the Tyre family.... I believe it is prudent for Beth and me to protect ourselves from a possible incident of the their doing. A letter like this has many implications with its undertones.... You're perfectly aware I've made no attempt to contact her or her family since I wrote a letter in mid–August telling her to not involve you, her children, and your children in her behavior.... Notice where Grace Tyre said that I breached confidentiality in mid–August. We all know Don's breach occurred before that time as did Dr. Tyre's.

....Accept your Christian responsibility, find your true faith, and do the right thing. Contact the hospital, Beth and I will go with you, and tell them the truth.... God will not fail you or your family....

John and Beth

My final, perhaps desperate, letter to the hospital medical director asking for help:

October 24

Dear Dr. Myers:

Thank you for your informative letter which states that Grace Tyre, MD is in good standing and I have received the "highest quality" of care. Once again, I am asking for a clarification as to University Medical Center's procedure for handling patient complaints. Am I being afforded the same procedural rights as other patients? UMC has never provided me with any manner to discuss my specific care concerns, although I requested such 6 months ago. (Reference my letter to Gold in April.)

If you review my records you will see four written prescriptions. Prescriptions written by Grace Tyre, MD. Dr. Grace Tyre made mistakes on two of them, or 50 percent.

The information in the enclosed letter from the Tyre's attorney stating that Don and Dr. Tyre, <u>both</u>, agree there has been a breach of confidentiality supports me. Her attorney's <u>specific</u> written acknowledgment emphasizing that I used the word "personal" in my letter, clearly sent in a way to protect my confidentiality in a small community in which <u>Dr</u>. Tyre is widely known as a psychiatrist, was very supportive, too. Dr. Myers, the exact word <u>"personal"</u> you used in your letter to prudently insure its <u>privacy</u> to me.

As I finish the first paragraph of this letter an ethical standard of the AMA comes to mind.

A physician shall respect the rights of patients, of colleagues, and of other health professions, and shall <u>safeguard patient confidences</u> within the constraints of the law.

Given the whole mix of events thus far, I wonder what prudent actions you, Dr. Gold, and other UMC staff have taken and are taking with Grace and Don Tyre and their children to safeguard my confidences. It is a fair question for me to ask since this breach happened several months ago.

Her attorney's letter infers that she and her husband may have special community privileges; privileges, which may infringe on my wife and myself. Perhaps you or your staff can define what you consider to be my freedom boundaries in various community settings such as a small social gathering in which Beth and I, Don, Dr. Tyre, and their children are attending or one in which there are common acquaintances. Dr. Tyre is under your employment jurisdiction and this matter, which her attorney specifically attaches to the quality of my care at UMC and our prior therapeutic relationship at UMC, needs to be addressed by University Medical Center. Further, this raises a rather troubling question in my mind: Can a therapist breach a patient's confidentiality by her non-verbal behavior actions towards him/her?

Prudently, I must continue to respond to the second part of her attorney's letter and why, also, I am asking you to define this community social structure. Much of the following information has been referenced in a prior letter to Dr. Gold. Once again, in my entire <u>lifetime</u> I have <u>never</u> spoken a word to Dr. Tyre's husband, nor to two of her sons. I have spoken two times to Dr. Tyre since last February. One time in the VA parking lot when I said, "Hello," and a second time when she was working in her garden and I said, "Good Evening." Her oldest son, I spoke with at my church picnic and when he came to <u>my</u> house. I haven't spoken to any Tyre since July. Also 8 weeks ago Beth and I stopped our occasional walk on Kennite township's road, Old Oak Road, after her husband

and a friend laughed and pointed at us as we walked down the public street. Beth was embarrassed, so we changed our walking pattern, and now take a more difficult walk.

What is troubling in this matter is that the Tyre's travel across our property several times a week, and have been doing so since my arrival in July. I question why Grace Tyre through her attorney's letter hasn't told me how <u>she has been and is safeguarding my patient confidences</u> when they are operating in my own backyard, as one might say. Certainly she is aware that her children have been playing on or around my property.

I guess what I am wondering once again as I write the above. Must a breach of confidentiality be verbal and if not, does the <u>physical or behavioral</u> manner in which a psychiatrist and others act toward a patient also represent <u>breaches</u> of confidentiality. Such thinking is troubling thinking in a small community like Kennite. I also thought her letter would have mentioned that Tyre family members travel daily across my property.

Of course the most troubling issue I have saved until last. Why is Dr. Grace Tyre mentioning <u>any</u> aspect of my psychiatric history to others. Her lawyer has stated I have received the "highest standards of professional care." You know, lawyers are very careful with their words. He, <u>himself</u>, states it. Dr. Tyre continues to raise serious questions in my mind regarding this <u>administrative UMC</u> matter.

Her attorney's reference to my therapy relationship with Dr. Tyre is inaccurate. After approximately 28 sessions with Dr. Tyre I asked Dr. Barber to investigate the quality of therapy I had been receiving. Dr. Tyre responded to my complaint in a manner which I had felt was inappropriate, so I left her therapy. Dr. Tyre and I shook hands when we parted and I left on good terms as noted by her own comment. After this we spoke on the telephone two or three times and we had a nice conversation about snowshoeing and therapeutic issues when Grace called me in Colorado last winter.

I have a right of confidentiality and privacy in this matter. <u>I have only asked that matters concerning my care be</u>

administratively reviewed by University Medical Center.

Finally the information enclosed in this letter is personal in nature so unless required by law I expect it not to be shared with Dr. Tyre. If by law you must, I expect to be notified of this action.

It is my understanding that senior claims representatives at AIG are attorneys by training.

John I. Lynch, Ed.D.

The pastor and Deacons reply to my letter. I believe he broke his obligation of pastoral confidentiality that he owed to Beth and me:

November 11

Dear John and Beth,

I am writing in response to our conversation on the afternoon of October 1 and John's letter of October 18, 1996. In light of the circumstances surrounding your conflict with the Tyres and my families friendship with their family I obviously am not the one to help you.... We do not intend to disrupt our continuing Christian witness to their family because of this situation....Just call the Deacons....

....we do not see how we have done you any wrong. We simply honored a request the Tyres made of us in confidence.

Pastor Hendrick

Dr. Gold's final word:

6 December

Dear Dr. Lynch:

Your October 24, 1996 letter addressed to Dr. Myers was referred to me. I have thoroughly reviewed your care in the University Medical Center Department of Psychiatry. I also met with you, personally, to review your concerns. Your care has been completely appropriate.

As has been previously communicated to you, your claim

of "breach of confidentiality" and your subsequent claims regarding your care have been referred to AIG Claim Services, Inc. and Mr. Matthew Wilson. This is standard Medical Center policy and we retain this independent firm to investigate claims of this type. Unfortunately, I am told your lack of cooperation with his investigation has resulted in a lack of progress that is not of our doing. I am referring your additional complaint letter to Mr. Wilson who has been assigned to investigate these claims.

I have been made aware that as part of Mr. Wilson's investigation, an independent psychiatric review/consult has been obtained. *That psychiatrist is of the opinion that your care was entirely appropriate, beneficial and that no breach of confidentiality occurred.*

I strongly recommend that you contact Mr. Wilson if you wish any additional follow-up on these complaints. If you do not wish to confer with Mr. Wilson, then I suggest you contact an attorney and pursue whatever other legal remedies you believe you have.

Any further correspondence regarding these issues will simply be forwarded to Mr. Wilson for necessary follow up.

Dr. Gold, Professor of Psychiatry and
Medicine, Chairman Psychiatry

After reading the letter, I said to Beth, "An independent psychiatrist made this judgement on expunged records which said nothing. I have a letter from Dr. Tyre telling me that all other records, except the set I was sent had been destroyed." The wisdom of my self–appeal failed as I went on to find a rationale for their misrepresentations.

"And the Medical Records department wrote you a note saying there were no more records," Beth added.

"It's sure a message for others," I said, dejectedly, "Just imagine what psychiatry's standard level of care must be, if I received the best." There's a long silence, then I remark with appropriate philosophical cynicism. "In psychiatry 'spin doctoring' is their moral category. And worst of all they convince others they're 'spinning' for altruistic reasons!"

Introduction to Part II

I suppose it had to end. It had been a curious hiatus, unimaginable to me at the beginning—first of all my OCD healing. Second, and even more surprising, my finding a therapist who looked and acted like my childhood mother. Within our therapeutic madness I lost myself only to find myself through God. Sure the haphazardness of what happened may appear absurd, but the outcome can't be denied. Today, my relationship with my parents has improved. I am active in a small Christian church, and I play tennis and write. For me, things have turned out just fine. But how does my experience help others?

This question encouraged me to write the last two chapters. I felt compelled to investigate the psychiatric and mental health systems to find out if I had been an isolated case. Chapter twenty presents my review. Here, experts who have been calling for change provide you with caveats.

Chapter twenty one is a personal chapter in which I give my recommendations for healing. I've entitled it, "God as Your Therapist."

CHAPTER 20

Therapeutic Madness for Others?

Introduction

After completing my manuscript, I reflected on my frightful therapeutic experience and wondered if I had gone to the quick of psychiatry: this disturbing thought thorned my conscience for many months. Even though my outcome had been successful and I survived this therapeutic experience, I realized there were many psychiatric patients who were less resourceful and resilient than I, and, perhaps, they needed to be forewarned and given another choice: my relationship with God had strengthened and protected me, I had a self of iron, and a wonderfully supportive wife; and even, with all these things my psychiatrist brought me to the edge and encouraged me to become an inpatient. I barely made it out! Clearly, I felt compelled to find out if I was the exception or the rule before concluding this book with a final message. So, I decided to answer three substantive questions in my review: what kind of psychological profiles did psychiatrists possess? what were their acceptable standards of conduct? what were the outcomes of those who turned their minds over to them?

I read a lot during the next several months and learned much about the mental health system and the people in it. In fairness to all I had no conclusions when I began. Not unexpectedly, I reviewed the professionally documented anti-mental health books initially. These books, written by therapists and abused ex-patients, were "engrossing" and "disturbing" and pointed to problems and dangers in the system much greater than I had ever imagined even given the extent of my therapeutic experience. It didn't take me long to realize how very fortunate I was to survive, undamaged, the "therapeutic abyss" these learned professionals described.

Frightfully, I discovered that "unsubstantiated and damaging diagnoses" are commonly given and often leaked, and that institutionalized patients' constitutional rights are taken away. These critics didn't take extreme positions and certainly weren't radicals, and their information was carefully documented and compelling. The mental health system is dominating and resourceful. Probably, they will dismiss me as having worthless and inaccurate conclusions even though I guardedly formulated this chapter. They may say I am a disgruntled ex–patient: maybe even give me a "loudly" whispered diagnosis, or there's the "a few rotten apples in every barrel" argument. My answer to their accusations and arguments, I determined, had to go beyond apple identification and defending myself so I thoughtfully and factually prepared the following literature review.

Literature Review

The Jewish theologian Martin Buber wrote about the "I" and "It" human relationship where the "I" sees the other person, the "It," as subhuman, worth little, and an inanimate object, even though the "I" may operate under a pretense of civility, friendliness, or caring. As Dr. M. Scott Peck, psychiatrist, notes in his book, *A World Waiting to be Born*, these relationships without dignity are perfectly virtuous in certain organizations.

Ferenczi, a student of Freud, clearly identifies the analytical "I"—"It" relationship when he writes, "Analysis is an easy opportunity to carry out purely selfish, unscrupulous, immoral, even criminal acts, and a chance to act out such behavior guiltlessly; for example, feeling a power over the numbers of helplessly worshipful patients who admire the analyst unreservedly, feeling sadistic pleasure in their suffering and their helplessness, and having no concern for how long the analysis lasts, in fact, the tendency to prolong it for purely financial reasons...," and, "as a result of infantile experiences created by the analyst it becomes impossible for patients to detach themselves from the analysis even after long and unsuccessful work...just as it is impossible for a child to run away from home, because, left on its own, it would feel helpless." Dr. Jeffrey Masson, past Director of the Freud Archives, in his book *Against Therapy* states, "the autocratic therapeutic structure serves only the interests of the all knowing therapist. The psychotherapist is superior, the patient always inferior. The patient cannot approach the psychotherapist without being bidden. The patient cannot question the psychotherapist. The psychotherapist decides how much time the patient can spend in his/her presence...."

The case of Psychiatrist John Rosen, who insisted he loved his patients, demonstrates a dynamic "I"—"It" therapeutic relationship. Dr. Rosen, a prominent psychiatrist and professor of psychiatry, who had been much praised by fellow psychiatrists for his "discoveries," surrendered his medical license in Pennsylvania for seventy–seven violations of the Medical Practices Act. Yet, according to Jeffrey Masson and others, "there is nothing unusual about what he did to his patients. In many other disguises, this kind of treatment goes undetected in thousands of psychiatric institutions throughout the United States. Indeed, far worse things happen on a daily basis." Following is a dialogue from one of Rosen's research papers printed for his colleagues:

Patient:	I was born a Jew.
Rosen:	Who cares?
Patient:	So you're probably the crazy one.
Rosen:	No, you're the crazy one.
Patient:	I know. How do you go about curing it?
Rosen:	Well, I'm a psychiatrist and I know how to cure.
Patient:	How do you do it?
Rosen:	By talking.
Patient:	Go ahead and talk.
Rosen:	I'm trying to find out what made you crazy.

Patient:	I think your mother did it.
	I was nervous all the time.
Rosen:	I know. I don't think your mother cared for you.

....

Rosen:	I don't like a liar.
Patient:	No, I don't lie. Why would I lie to you?
Rosen:	Because you want to hide the fact that you were crazy.

In another article by Rosen, *The Survival Function of Schizophrenia,* published in the bulletin of the Menninger Clinic, he writes: "Come on. No more fucking. I added, 'no more fucking' which is an interpretation on the genital level, rather than, 'no more rocking,'.... He, then, tells the patient that she can suck his thumb:

Rosen:	You can keep it there as long as you want. It's all right. It's all right. Do you get pleasure from it?
Patient:	Yes.
Rosen:	Is it exciting?
Patient:	Yes. Yes. Hard. Hard. Hard. Hard....
Rosen:	I am your mother now and I will permit you to do whatever you want."

Rosen had strong support as he practiced this kind of psychiatry. P. Spurgeon English, for many years chairman of the Department of Psychiatry at Temple University School of Medicine, in *Introduction to Psychiatry*, a widely used textbook, praised Rosen and his innovative methods of treatment.

Dr. Robert Baker, professor emeritus of psychology at the University of Kentucky, in his book, *Mind Games: Are We Obsessed With Therapy?* concludes, "the history of psychotherapy is marked by incompetence, inhumane and immoral treatment, and a total misunderstanding of human beings."

Thomas Szasz, psychiatrist and longtime critic of the psychiatric system, in his book, *Ideology and Insanity: Essays on the Psychiatric Dehumanization of Man*, speaks to a system where "I" and "It" relationships are academically and professionally nurtured and where the outcome is the dehumanization of people.

Arguably, most professional acts are undertaken with a purpose, or at least a rationalization, that they are helping. Nonetheless, there are people for whom psychiatry is a means of misleading others, for they misuse its calling, its attractions, for their own destructive needs. In either case, however, "most psychiatrists," according to Dr. Baker, "are, unfortunately, neither scientists nor psychologists. Instead, they are actually poorly trained medical technicians who, at the moment, are incapable of dealing adequately with many—if not most— of the various psychological disorders experienced by the public. Freudian theory is an approach even more seriously flawed, fallacious, and inadequate than the medical model. Today psychiatrists are pill-pushers or analysts. Neither approach is effective or relevant...."

R. Webster in his book, *Why Freud was Wrong: Sin, Science...*, states that Freud, the historical myth creator, desperate for academic glory, claimed to have found the cure for morphine addiction: substitution by cocaine which, he asserted, was non–addictive. He based this on a single case and published a paper claiming it. The n=1 case was established in psychiatry: obviously, the sign of a flawed researcher, theorist, and ethical person. Professor R. C. Tallis supports this view and writes, "Freud as a scientist, metapsychologist, and diagnostician of society emerges as a quack." He points to the story of a little girl whose abdominal pains Freud had been treating as an "unmistakable" hysteria who died of abdominal lymphoma two months after he had treated her. Freud defended himself robustly, claiming to have dealt satisfactorily with the situation. He just refused to accept responsibility, a current day, successful, political strategy. Despite disturbing examples like these, Freud's theories pervade therapy and counseling methodologies.

Medawar in the New York Review of Books, chillingly

acknowledges that Freud's theory is the "most stupendous intellectual confidence trick of the twentieth century." Another historical myth creator psychiatrist Hermann Oppenheim in his series on children's mental disturbances said, "children should not be allowed to demonstrate strong emotions of any kind, either positive or negative...." A book by Robyn Dawes, *House of Cards or Terrence Campell's Beware the Talking Cure: Psychotherapy May Be Hazardous to Your Mental Health,* calls attention to the large number of commonly held myths within psychology that have little or no supporting evidence.

Myth practice is most observable in fringe therapies, perhaps, because financial power is weaker causing public relation efforts to be less persuasive. Margaret Singer, clinical psychologist and emeritus adjunct professor at University of California at Berkeley, and Janja Lalich discuss therapies such as, alien abduction, inner child work, and flower essence in their book *Crazy Therapies*. They relate stories of the countless individuals who have turned over their innermost thoughts to trusted therapists, only to be exploited. There has been an explosion of therapies, at least 250 different ones now exist according to Richie Herink, editor of *The Psychotherapy Handbook: A to Z Guide.*

The proliferation of therapies has come about because of therapist proliferation. Between 1955 and 1980 the number of psychiatrists per population doubled, and between 1970 and 1990 the number of psychologists increased from less than 30,000 to more than 191,000 (not counting marriage, religious, family counselors, and social workers). Of course, more therapists generate more patients. Dr. Baker in his book, *Mind Games: Are We Obsessed with Therapy* clearly tells us how patients are recruited, "all of us are sick, dysfunctional, neurotic, addicted, maladjusted, depressed, compulsive, codependent, disconnected, spiritually lost, disaffected, anxious, phobic, and so on. We are all victims of our time, our genetic inheritance..., moral, sexual, economic. But in this stygian atmosphere of doom there is at least a ray of hope:

psychotherapy," and other therapies, I might add.

In a March 17, 1993 New York Times article, we see how the media acts as publicizer for the mental health system, not a watch guard. Coleman, the article's author, writes, "while approximately 52 million adults in the United State—more than 1 in 4 suffer from some mental disorder at some point during a year, only 28 percent of them seek help according to the most comprehensive study of the nation's mental health ever conducted." And the experts keep repeating the message to us. Ronald C Kessler, sociology professor, published a study in the *Archives of General Psychiatry* revealing that almost 50 percent of the American population experience mental illness at some time, one third are afflicted each year. James J. Judson and Harrison G. Pope, psychiatrists, published a 1990 article in the American Journal of Psychiatry stating that they are able to identify a new mental illness which affects approximately one-third of the world's population. These messages are gladly disseminated by our media, foundations, churches, educational institutions, and governmental agencies.

Frederick Crews, Professor Emeritus UC Berkley, from *The Revenge of the Repressed*, in the New York Review of books, part I, Nov 17, 1994, gives us a prospective for victims and states, "by 1988 1,000,000 families have been estimated to be affected by therapist–inspired charges of sexual molestation. Now the all–knowing autocratic therapist is able to persuade individuals they suffered sexual abuse of which they have no recollection." There's also the sexual abuse directly attributable to the therapist.

Pamela Sutherland, Attorney at Law, in an article about professional sexual abuse, notes that in one self–reporting survey that as high as 13.7 percent of male (therapists responding) and 3.1 of female respondents "admitted" engaging in some form of erotic contact with at least one patient. Pope and Bouhoutsos reported that 15 percent of therapists have had sexual contact with their patients. And we must remember, these are the number of therapists willing to respond. Of course, the problem with such surveys is that they are taken of offenders. Imagine attempting to find out how many men have raped by asking nonconvicted rapists whether they are guilty of rape.

Another survey of practicing therapists found that 70 percent are aware of at least one patient who has been a sexual victim of a previous therapist. The media seldom reports or follows–up such cases. Contrarily, when an Army sergeant has consensual sex with several recruits, "it's a national scandal," and the media screams for retribution and change.

On rare occasions sexually abused patients do sue, but if the case is settled out of court it is not considered a malpractice judgement against the therapist. Not many would argue, the legal system offers substantially more protection for the therapist than the victimized patient. Still, there are a few stories of victims gaining back a modicum of self–respect. For example, Ellen Plaisl and others brought suit against her psychiatrist who surrendered his license before the court, but, perhaps, went to another state to practice. Margaret Singer in *Crazy Therapies* presents Ellen's and her psychiatrist's disturbing dialogue:

Psychiatrist:	"You scum," he muttered slowly.... "I'm thinking of throwing you out of here."
Ellen:	I knelt on the floor.... "Please don't throw me out." I whispered in desperation..."I'm sorry. Really sorry. I'll do anything to make it up to you, but please, please don't throw me out."
Psychiatrist:	"You're not even half the woman I thought you were and I didn't think you were much to start with.... You violated my first rule. You didn't tell me everything that was going on inside your head.... And all this over a little sex.... Your future is over unless I agree to continue seeing you...."

Ellen: "I know," I replied in a whisper. I really
               believed it.

This occurred because she went to another psychiatrist to
get away from him, and he informed his colleague about it.

Even today sex with patients is still promoted within the
profession. Susan Baur, clinical psychologist, in her book,
The Intimate Hour: Love and Sex in Psychotherapy, asserts
that the primary obligation of a therapist to a patient is to cure
him or her: if this means initiating a love/sex liaison, so be it.
Dr. Baur contends that ethical liaison in the form of love
between doctor and patient is the key to a positive therapeutic
outcome. Be it same sex or different sex relationships. Martin
Shepard in his book, *The Love Treatment,* took the position
that many *women* would benefit by having sexual liaisons
with their therapists.

Dr. Singer identifies the extent of sex under the guise of
therapy and writes, "research over the past several decades
has shown that anywhere from 33 to 80 percent of those
therapists who instigate sexual encounters with patients tend
to repeat their unethical behavior with more than one patient.
This happens because...emotionally the patient is often no
longer wanted..., because another appealing patient has been
found. Even if a patient/victim confides this to another
therapist, he/she may find there is a kind of professional
bonding and probably will receive little comfort,
understanding, or help from the new therapist." The presented
statistics show that over 30,000 patients have been sexually
exploited, and their numbers are increasing every day because
therapists won't testify against their "colleagues."

In his popular book, *Sexual Exploitation in Professional
Relationships,* Glen Gabbard, psychiatrist, points to the
patient damage, "Incest victims and those who have been
sexually exploited by professionals (therapists) have
remarkably similar symptoms: shame, intense guilt, feelings
of isolation,...forced silence,...suicidal and self destructive
behavior."

Derek Jeu and others have also written about dire

consequences for sexually abused patients in their book, *Patients As Victims: Sexual Abuse in Psychotherapy and Counseling.* A book by Herbert Strean, professor emeritus, Rutgers University, titled, *Therapist's Who Have Sex With Their Patients: Treatment and Recovery,* reviews this serious problem, too.

There are a number of personal accounts such as the one Lucy Freeman presents in *Betrayal: The True Story of the First Woman to Successfully Sue Her Psychiatrist for Using Sex in the Guise of Therapy,* and *Sex in the Therapy Hour*: *A Case of Professional Incest* by Carolyn Bates. But it is not easy to prove such behavior as Dr. Baker reasons, "because of Medical Deism and the power and prestige of the offending physician, it is very difficult indeed to make charges of wrong–doing hold up in court. You are advised to work closely with your local prosecutor and wear a wire."

A book by Eileen McNamara, an investigative reporter with the Boston Globe, called *Breakdown: Sex Suicide, and the Harvard Psychiatrist,* is quite compelling and provides an inside look into psychiatry's lethal failure to distinguish quackery. It is a dramatic example of what can happen when a male patient's vulnerability and a female doctor's fantasies play out to a fatal outcome. Dr. Strean also speaks of this case in his book. He reports that Dr. Margaret Bean-Bayog, psychiatrist, associated with the Harvard Medical School spoke to her patient, Paul Lozano, such words as, *"I'm your mom, and I love you, and you love me very much...."*

According to Dr. Baker, the Psychiatric Association ethics committee at one time even seriously considered ignoring patient–doctor relations, but now see it as a necessary evil. Nevertheless, the APA holds the belief that some—even many—offenders can be rehabilitated with one to five years of probationary supervision. But patients are never informed of a therapist's probation. California guidelines warn patients to be suspicious when a therapist *gives suggestive looks, stands or sits too close.* Jeanine Grobe, editor, in her book, *Beyond Bedlam: Contemporary Women Psychiatric Survivors*

Speak Out, alludes to another victimization, "the torture of those who have been labeled 'mentally ill.'" These labels are mostly derived from the Diagnostic and Statistical Manual, DSM.

Psychiatrists, therapists, and social workers are required to use the DSM for consistency in diagnosing patients and for insurer reimbursements. It has a catchy title but when held accountable as a scientific work, it fails miserably. For example, several years ago homosexuality was considered a mental disease. Then, the 1973 DSM dropped it. The switch from disease to individual choice shows that "social agreement," rather than "scientific evidence" is the determiner. Stuart A. Kirk and Herb Kutchins, following up on their excellent 1992 book *The Selling of the DSM: The Rhetoric of Science in Psychiatry*, gave a scathing review of the DSM-IV in the National Psychologist and call it—a travesty. The DSM's inherent problem is that it applies no coherent standard of what constitutes a mental disorder. It diagnoses so many ordinary kinds of behavior as psychiatric disorders that 50 percent of the American population is now mentally ill. Even poor spelling, grammar, and punctuation is now a disease: Code 215.2, Disorder of Written Expression. Not only is this totally asinine, but it also classifies children who argue with adults, lose their tempers, refuse to obey rules, blame others; and act touchy, angry, or spiteful as mentally ill: Code 313.81, Appositional Defiant Disorder. This is stupid and very dangerous.

Late Luteal Phase Dysphonic Disorder, formally known as the Premenstrual Dysphoric Disorder, a depression associated with hormonal changes during the menstrual cycle was added in the DSM–IV—pathologizing a normal experience (PMS). The mere fact that this category is included and regarded as a "disease" speaks volumes about the absurdity of psychiatric thinking and the "diseasing" of America. A book by Anne Figert, *Women and the Ownership of PMS: The Structuring of a Psychiatric Disorder (Social Problems and Social Issues)*, discusses this issue in detail.

Dr. Paula Caplan, psychologist and former consultant to those who constructed the Diagnostic and Statistical Manual of Mental Disorders in her book, *They Say You're Crazy: How the World's Most Powerful Psychiatrists Decide Who's Normal*, states that personal biases behind it are often masquerading as solid science and truth. She debunks the intimidating psychobabble and pronouncements of the American Psychiatric Association. And as the Cleveland Plain Dealer comments in a review of her book: "Gives us a fighting chance to avoid becoming victims of the mental health establishment."

J. Kovel in his article, *A Critique of the DSM-III, Research in Law, Deviance & Social Control*, remarks that the medieval witch trials show a much higher interrater reliability than any of the DSM categories and we definitely do not impute any validity to those social diagnoses. He also notes that validity requires that the variable or item be highly correlated with a known measure such as clinical diagnosis in medical records. And states, "Biopsychiatry, nevertheless, is satisfied with the fact that DSM–II–R and DSM–IV have been widely accepted by courts, prisons, clinics, and third–party payers. This, according to the biopsychiatrists, is evidence of a major scientific breakthrough." Why? Because when the institutions accept the beliefs and practices of any scientific model, a form of scientific knowledge has been created. This is not, however, the way the rest of the scientific world defines validity.

In 1959, the highly respected psychiatrist and psychoanalyst Karl Menninger stated, "Diagnosis in the sense in which we doctors have used it for so many years is not only relatively useless in many cases, it is an inaccurate, misleading, and a philosophically false predication." In his book, *Nobody's Victim, Freedom From Therapy and Recovery*, Christopher McCullough, analyst, says, "No longer are we allowed to have interesting personality quirks or oddities. Psychopathological terms are given to us." With a hefty price tag, I might add.

The OCD Foundation newsletter of April 1997 presents a staff article titled *Seinfeld Under a 'Brain Scan,' Your Everyday Obsessives* and is based on the book, *Shadow Syndromes,* by John Ratey, psychiatrist, and Catherine Johnson which supports the Freudian dictum that no one is truly normal.... Their book points out that new brain–scanning techniques lend credence to the belief that most if not all people possess at least one or more neurochemical imperfections.... "Jerry is even too squeamish to eat animal meat.... Shade 'victims' Jerry, George, Elaine, and Kramer maybe kissin' cousins to even the severest OCD sufferers." The OCD Foundation is controlled by the drug companies and psychiatry, although they would never admit this. The article goes on to say, "this newly defined syndrome, *Shadow Syndrome*, may sharply increase estimates of how many in the general population are *biochemically imperfect*. By so doing, it intensifies the spotlight on OCD and related problems, which could be a boom to the pharmaceutical industry."

Pharmapsychiatry

The pharmaceutical industry is big and rich and much like the industrial trusts of the early 1900's its influence over the media, government, and foundations is enormous. Drug consumers, therefore, must use extreme caution when taking medication. In a study according to the FDA, 1978, 1.5 million Americans were hospitalized as a result of side effects from prescription drugs and 30 percent of all people hospitalized were further damaged by medication. Every year, an estimated 140,000 Americans are killed because of prescription drug consumption while one in seven hospital beds are taken up by patient's suffering from adverse reaction according to Dr. Baker.

Dr. Thomas Szasz, psychiatrist, provides an historical prospective of the use of drugs in psychiatry in his book, *Cruel Compassion, Psychiatric Control of Society's Unwanted*: "During the years immediately following the war (WWII) psychiatry was an odd couple, one partner warehousing impoverished nonproducers in snake pits, the other giving dynamic psychotherapy to successful producers in his private office. Drugs and de-institutionalization rescued this absurd combination of somatic therapy in the hospital and psychotherapy in the office by transforming both into a homogenized biological–coercive psychiatry plus talk therapy."

In psychiatry, Dr. Baker notes: "All mental disorders and 'diseases' were—and currently are—assumed to be due to a disorder of brain metabolism. Then, by straightening out the faulty metabolism the patient will also be straightened out. To this end psychiatrists administer potent mind altering drugs." Ron Liefer, psychiatrist, adds, "We spend billions of dollars to prevent people from using marijuana and on the other hand force a whole population of other people to take these other drugs which have no redeeming effects and which are quite dangerous."

Catherine Odette gives her drug testament in *Beyond Bedlam, Contemporary Women Psychiatric Survivors Speak Out,* "For almost 15 years I lived in state hospitals receiving treatment for my psychiatric disability. I received drugs as part of my treatment. The levels of Thorazine and Stelazine I was taking are now considered toxic.... My mind was a toxic dump. I was chemically strait jacketed, almost incapable of thought. Often, because I tried to refuse these drugs, they were forced into my body. I knew, even in the nearly unconscious state of my toxic wasteland that those drugs were wrong and were damaging me." Peter Breggin in his book, *Psychiatric Drugs: Hazards to the Brain,* debunks the myth that psychiatric drugs are designed to cure mental diseases and says many only induce a state of psychic indifference, "zombiism."

The war on illegal drugs began decades ago, but there is no war to help people get off legalized drugs. According to best estimates, the antianxiety drugs account for 250 to 300 million prescriptions a year which means over sixty doses for every man, woman, and child in the nation. Take Prozac for example. The FDA received 16,583 reports of adverse reactions to Prozac between 1987 and 1991. Robert A King, assistant professor of child psychiatry at the Yale Medical School and author of numerous studies suggesting a link between Prozac and suicide states, "The moral of the story is that people who are on it must be followed closely, and people shouldn't be on it for trivial reasons." In 1952 the American Psychiatric Association recognized 110 discrete mental illnesses, today there are 220. More disorders equals higher drug sales and talk therapy.

The decade of the 90's may be called the decade of nonaccountabilty for many bureaucratic systems and the 20th century may be called the century of nonaccountability for mental health. In an important essay in *Cohen's Challenging the Therapeutic State*, Ken Barney states that in spite of three decades of trenchant critique and rights advocacy nothing has had any effect on either the language or the basic operations of the mental health system. Janet Gotkin's story, *Too Much Anger, Too Many Tears*, was published in 1975 and gives us "why" insight. Her book was hailed by The New York Times Book Review as "one of the most important documents in the history of psychiatry." Still, it was not reviewed in a single national publication outside the library field. No major book club accepted it, most network talk shows refused to have her speak. "Psychiatry launched considerable efforts to discredit me." Ms. Gotkin also said: "that she believes the power of the personal narrative is so monumental that over the years enormous efforts have been launched to undermine the veracity of people who would tell the truth." As Dr. Barney observes, "Oppressive and dehumanizing practices continue unchanged. Biomedical reductionism retains its great appeal."

Dr. Baker agrees and writes, "Despite the weakness of psychiatric theory and the uncertainty of the biopsychiatrists' medical approach, their arrogance and megalomanic air of competence has continued unabated. In this regard they have been aided and abetted by an uncritical media." Anne Boedecker, a private practitioner, recently has written in the

National Psychologist, "as a profession we have let 'therapy' grow unchecked and unregulated. Therapists used to justify sexual involvement..., most therapy works from theory not research..., there is no real screening process for preventing destructive people from becoming therapists..., the mental health field is poorly regulated."

Money creates power, and this power creates control and nonaccountability in solidified structures. Ekstein and Wallerstein in their book, *Teaching and Learning of Psychotherapy*, identify the importance of the solidifying indoctrination process for every practitioner: "Professional training, if it truly succeeds, leads to a psychological amalgamation of the person with the function that he is to perform. We speak not of having a job, but of being a member of a profession.... The sense of professional identity is an essential attribute in a profession such as psychotherapy, and its acquisition must be considered one of the important training goals." Jeffrey Masson writes to this issue and says, "In short, one is learning to become a loyal member of a select group. A natural response to criticism is to attack the critic because loyalty to one's profession is considered essential."

Adam Phillips, analyst, in his book, *Terror and Expert*, says his colleagues talk knowingly like they are in a *cult*.... (an autocratic structure represented by high levels of power, authority, control, and member protection). They forget, Phillips remarks, they (his colleagues) are telling stories about other stories and that all stories are subject to an unknowable multiplicity of interpretations. Dr. Baker carries this idea of a cult mentality farther and says this is a totally neglected aspect of psychotherapy. He states only a cultist structure could protect the large number of psychotherapists who have managed to violate every ethical rule and principle in the practice of their craft and wind up ruining their client's lives. In a paper titled, *Some Hazzards of the Therapeutic Relationship*, the Temerlins painfully describe precisely how charismatic psychotherapists are able to manipulate the therapeutic relationship and produce groups that function like destructive religious cults. Dr. Baker considers religiously inspired psychotherapists to be more dangerous.

In *Madness, Heresy and the Rumor of Angels: The Revolt Against The Mental Health System*, a book by Dr. Seth Farber, the author, discusses psychotherapy dissent with Ron Leifer, psychiatrist:

Farber: It's amazing when you think of the parallel between them attempting to suppress dissident psychiatrists, how it parallels the attempt to put mental patients in mental hospitals.

Liefer: That's why I say I'm a victim of psychiatry. Then they call you by psychiatric names. They began to tell unfounded stories about Szasz. To this day, he still has a reputation in psychiatry as being mentally ill. That's how they dismiss him.

Garth Wood's book, *The Myth of Neurosis*: *Overcoming the Illness Excuse*, reaffirms Liefer's position, "when a therapist doesn't want to deal with a patient, he/she gives the patient a diagnosis and packing notice."

Self–Help is Real Help

Ralph Waldo Emerson advises that the path away from victimization is self-reliance, the process by which your mind is turned over to itself. St. Augustine in his *Confessions*, and Pascal in his *Mind on Fire: A Christian's Character Before God*, and more recently the *Diaries of Anais Nin* give testament to self–reliance through journal writing. All operated outside a formal analytical setting. Karen Horney the famous psychiatrist in her book, *Self–Analysis,* also supports the concept of an analysis without a therapist. Within journal writing, times of exaltation and despair, love and anger, success and failure, righteousness and sin can crystalize and cause the formation of a discernable self and disparate inner movement. Life will become easier.

Dr. Baker in *Mind Games: Are We Obsessed With Therapy*, recommends other healing processes in caring for oneself but first of all reminds us " your mental disorder—if you really have one—is most likely an emotional disorder: socially and environmentally engendered; due to bad luck, injustice, and mistreatment, or to faulty learning and thinking and a lack of adequate coping strategies and techniques. It cannot be corrected or straightened out by a pill! He provides a do-it-yourself guide: friends, no drugs, avoid TV,...."

Self–healing from the theological perspective has God at its center. Contrarily, Freud called religious beliefs, illusions. Szasz makes the argument that Freud practiced Judaism and was anti–gentile. Albert Ellis, prolific theorist and writer in his book, *Case Against Religion: A Psychotherapists View and the Case Against Religiosity*, speaks strongly against prayer and religion in healing and calls faith irrational thinking and emotional disturbance.

Of 3,777 articles published by four major psychiatry journals over five years, only three examine religion factors, according to Dr. Larson, a psychiatrist, at the National Institute of Health. Yet he has found 92 percent of studies over a twelve year period reported that faith strengthens mental health. Michael McManus in his newspaper column points to the reason for this happening. Here he notes that 21 percent of psychiatrists and 28 percent of clinical psychologists are admitted atheists or agnostics, and their numbers are increasing. Yet, 96 percent of Americans believe in God.

The Apostle James said, "Prayer offered in faith will make the sick person well." The National Institute of Religion and Health can provide over 300 studies supporting these words. Larry Dossey, M.D in his book, *Healing Words the Power of Prayer and Practice of Medicine*, has found more than 130 studies linking prayer with recoveries.

CHAPTER 21

God as Your Therapist

It has been two years since I completed my psychiatric experience with Grace; nevertheless, I have continued my therapy with God. Time has arrived for me to reflect on God's power as therapist and healer. Today, the limiting nature of my neurosis has left me, and I feel confident to address the compelling issue of healing with God: a process which exists for believers, nonbelievers, and atheists. These reflections will not contend with organized religion or Biblical references except for a few words and a few quotes. My intent is to communicate my inner healing experience. Your direction can be congruent with mine.

Unfortunately, Christianity doesn't equate with secular "peace of mind," as some might assume. Both Christians and non–Christians endure a host of neurotic difficulties, for example, anxiety disorders. Christians, to me, are better off in problematic neurotic states than are nonbelievers because Christians, to their good fortune, can always call on God to help them in troubled times and at death they find eternal life. One year ago Beth and I started attending church. Last winter in a small church we sang in the choir of 12, made many friends, and were given a farewell social reception when we headed north for the summer. They were a wonderful group of Christians, and we enjoyed worshiping with them. Nevertheless, I found within our northern and southern congregation many Christians who displayed and admitted to having troubled "neurotic" lives. Some of the most disturbing mental health was demonstrated by the two pastors.

Peace of mind and self realization through God is different from my Christian kinship with Him, and, perhaps, that explains why sorrowful mental health afflicts many Christians. Very early in life I was told that Christians were happy, contented people who had gained this peace through Bible reading, prayer, and formal church worship. By following these recommendations early in life, I formed a believing relationship with God, even within the turmoil of my young, emotionally traumatized life. Still, the "peace of mind" that the church so "boldly"assured never became my reality. If I hadn't constructed a new therapeutic relationship with God, I suspect that death in fragile mental health would have been my reality; nevertheless, if anyone, not just me, forms a therapeutic relationship with God then earthly "peace of mind" may become his or her truth. The Apostle Paul spoke of it when he said, "I have conquered the world."

It took me too many years to arrive at this conclusion. A prayerful and meditating relationship with God seemed unnecessary during most of my life. I had adopted and accepted sorrowful mental health. I rejected the notion of exploring my childhood self because I knew it would be a bitter and antagonizing experience: one that should be avoided at all cost, even though, I knew my difficulties festered within that childhood emotional framework. Like many people, the unknown inner self scared me. Not knowing myself, and it should be noted here that God is part of that inner self, constricted my mind and behaviors.

God's promise is, "Ye shall seek Me, and find Me, when ye shall search for Me with all your heart." Jeremiah 29:13. I tried to make this a truth by reading the Bible and praying on occasion, but for most of my life the distance between God and myself was great and I now know why! My search for God had been in the wrong places and my heart wasn't in it. I never realized that God existed within my "self," and the further I went into the self the more of God I'd find. St. Augustine realized this but for most of my life I didn't. The worldly was my allure and I looked for God there. I thought of God as a miracle maker and someone who existed in heaven and came and went in my life. Such thinking led to self–centered prayer. I prayed, as too many Christians do, for the material things of life: good health, good jobs, good times.

I found no therapeutic value in this kind of praying. Today, I am not surprised that God didn't act as my santa klaus and my mental health was lacking. There was little congruence between what I was and what He expected of me during this period.

When my psychiatric experience began with Grace, I envisioned the psychiatric process as an abyss, nevertheless, it seemed to be my only choice. I never thought of entering psychotherapy or behavioral therapy with God. That realization came only at the end of my therapy. Today, I realize that God is the most wonderful therapist. He never makes a therapeutic mistake or seeks His own gratification at my expense. God is available to me 24 hours a day, seven days a week; there's no 50 minute clock. God will meet with me as often as I need. I don't have to travel anywhere to do my therapy with Him because God is always with me. God, my therapist, loves me and cares what happens to me, and He won't give me "a you're not all right diagnosis" and harmful label. I can say anything to Him no matter how disturbing the words are to me. He understands my words because he knows all about me, though I realize His understanding will not always be His acceptance. God has his therapeutic rules, and these rules are rigidly set by Him.

In therapy with Grace I knew that God was with me, although I wasn't in any therapeutic program with Him. I felt His closeness when the pastor whom I sought help from bid me "farewell." Of course, when God came to me and gave me the strength to overcome my OCD, his presence was ardently felt. The uniqueness of my therapy drew me closer to God and I began to wonder if God had created a destiny for me. I began writing a self–analysis journal, although my writing quality was poor, and I didn't like to write. Grace embodied my mother's look and more importantly her behaviors. I found suppressed memories. I bought the only house for sale in a rural neighborhood where the pastor's family, my new next door neighbors, were best friends with Grace's family. I needed three letters to support my story and all three letters were sent to me: Grace's letter, Gold's letter, and Hendrick's letter. People entered and left my life at the right times.... Still, questions about what happened to me linger.

The most commanding question is: What role did Grace play in my healing process? Some will say I was infatuated with her, others, like I, will say that it was God's plan for me. Without doubt, Grace represented troubling images of others. Yet, all these images, people, were still alive and most were in my life. Perhaps, I found no healing in my attachments with them because I interacted with them through cognitive justification for feelings. When the cognitions changed the feelings changed and the confusion reigned. My emotional relationship with Grace was quite atypical: the emotions were natural and cognitive structures were limited. Throughout the early and middle time of my therapeutic experience, I believed that God wanted me to examine my emotional self without guilt feelings, and I had my astounding OCD improvement to support this conclusion, so I let the emotions cascade.

During the early part of my therapy, I meditated with God on occasion. But I wouldn't call it therapeutic meditation. I mostly asked Him to help me untangle the emotional turmoil in my life. Prayers were brief, several minutes at most. My emotions awakened by self-analysis writing commanded me into my inner self. Unexpectedly, as I went deeper and deeper into my innerself I encountered more and more of God. When I arrived at the essence of myself, the period after my swearing episode with Grace, I reached the God, that I had craved. I now understood my rightful self to God and that God wanted this new found self to mature with Him, "to be all I could be for Him, not me!"

From this point I began to view other minds with amazing discernment. The bonds of my neurosis had been cut and I could begin maturing, although I was emotionally fragile. Growth was slow, but surely forward. What had happened to me was quite remarkable and a blessing from God: **a blessing that I worked hard to maintain**. After my BPD diagnosis,

I realized it was time to leave this therapeutic madness with her and to begin rebuilding my life with God. Yes, emotional confusion did reign then, but I knew what to do! I left this therapy and went to my calling of writing this book.

Grace's appearance and behavior put me on the "fast" track to emotional exploration. Still, we humans can easily create emotional images in our minds. My emotional dynamics could have existed with other psychotherapists, I suspect. And I could have gone through a similar process with them. But this wouldn't be the way for me, today. God makes a matchless therapist to explore your emotions with. Clearly, I survived worldly therapy with Grace who encouraged me at the end to become an inpatient.... I almost turned my mind over to the wrong person.

It was sad that my experience with Dr. Tyre had to end as it did, but it did motivate me, initially, to write this book. I left Dr. Tyre confused but focused on forming a therapeutic relationship with God. Over the next year I therapeutically meditated with God about my writings and myself. Almost every night I meditated, drifting in and out of sleep, for an hour or two, sometimes longer. As I did, healing took place. All was not smooth, however, and there were days when emotional confusion reigned. When this happened I increased my therapy time with God which tired my mind and made my emotions raw. But the next day things were right and I knew I was healing. At the end of this year I adjudged myself a different emotional person. I had become strong and secure and self-confident with emotions. God had been the most inspiring therapist for me. I had healed enough to leave my formal therapy structure with Him and I began studying His word, the Bible. Here He gave me His plan for how my life should be led. During my intensive therapeutic year with God, I didn't read two verses of the Bible or attend church.

Today, if I had to do it over, I would select a different process. I would do two hours a day of self–analysis writings, three times a week, and I would do my psychotherapy with God at least three times a week mostly before bedtime, when

I awoke at night, and first thing in the morning. My innerself is quite near Him and me at these times. If I needed more therapy time then I would do more. A life anew is one well worth working for. I spent forty-five years trying to find my core self, so I wouldn't expect too rapid a change. I suspect at times I would want to run from myself and the emotions I was feeling, but I wouldn't because this is my healing medicine. I still meditate with God, on occasion, about my burdensome childhood. He's always available.

If you seek God and His therapy with all your heart, then you'll find him. I define the word heart to mean, you want to know Him. When you know God you'll know that he has high expectations for you. If your heart lies in the world and self justification, then it may be a long road for you to travel to find him. Nevertheless, what is your other option: the worldly abyss of psychotherapy and separation form God for eternity.

Final Reflections

Paul Johnston's book The Quest for God, speaks to God being in us and to self reliance: "Each of us has this individual relationship with our creator and nothing can take it away from us. Each of us can lose our soul and each can save it." It is an undoubted and possible tragic fact as Pascal remarks, 'On mourra seul,' we die alone. We come to individual judgement.

James Joyce, in his classic work, *A Portrait of the Artist as a Young Man*, compellingly speaks to our final outcome, eternity.

"....You have often seen the sand on the seashore. How fine are its tiny grains! Now imagine a mountain of that sand, a million miles high, reaching from the earth to the farthest heavens, and a million miles broad, extending to remotest space, and a million miles in thickness: and imagine such an enormous mass of countless particles of sand multiplied as often as there are leaves in the forest, drops of water in the mighty ocean, feathers on birds, scales on fish, hairs on animals, atoms in the vast expanse of the air: and imagine that at the end of every million years a little bird came to that mountain and carried away in its beak a tiny grain of sand. How many millions upon millions of centuries would pass before that bird had carried away even a square foot of that mountain, how may eons upon eons of ages before it had carried away all. Yet at the end of that immense stretch of time not even could one instant of eternity could be said to have ended. At the end of all those billions of trillions of years eternity would have scarcely begun, and if...never to receive, even for an instant God's pardon, ever to suffer, never to enjoy, ever to be dammed... ever, never, ever, never...."

Closing Thoughts

I searched my inner psyche for the oneness of God and self following an aphorism of immense proportion "you'll never know God until you know yourself." There were journal entries about "this" and "that," my years with OCD, and my relationship with God, all referenced in this chapter. Writings could be clear, straightforward, and concise, "God would punish me...," or complex, symbolic and poetic: "This is a remembrance of a time gone by when my soul heard a far away sound, an almost lifeless dictate from a thing called fear.... A soul entombed in the site she laid undying in unhampered days gone by, and I listen to the moan of survival only from a perimeter for it is my entire presence, except for daily lassitude, for every element and organism it acts upon this presence." My personalized language to self–discovery.

> In a dark time, the eye begins to see.
> I meet my shadow in the deepening shade;
> I hear my echo in the echoing wood–
> A lord of nature weeping to a tree.

I live between the heron and the wren
Beasts of the hill and serpents of the den.
What's madness but nobility of soul
At odds with circumstance? The day's on fire!
I know the purity of pure despair
My shadow pinned against a sweating wall.
That place among the rocks—is it a cave,
Or winding path? The edge is what I have.
Dark, dark my light, and darker my desire.
My soul, like some heat-maddened summer fly,
Keeps buzzing at the sill. Which I is I?
A fallen man, I climb out of my fear.
The mind enters itself, and God the mind,
And one is One, free in the tearing wind.

(Roethke)

THE END

BIBLIOGRAPHY

Aftel, Mandy and Robin T. Iakoff. *When Talk Is Not Cheap. Or, How to Find the Right Therapist When You Don't Know Where to Begin.* New York: Warner Books, 1985.

Armstrong, Louise. *And They Call It Help. The Psychiatric Policing of America's Children.* MA: Wesley Publishing, 1993.

Baker, Robert A. *Hidden Memories: Voices and Visions from Within.* NY: Prometheus, 1992.

Baker, Robert A. *Mind Games: Are We Obsessed With Therapy?* NY: Prometheus, 1996.

Bates, Carolyn M. and Annette M. Brodsky. *Sex in the Therapy Hour: A Case of Professional Incest.* Guilford Press, 1993.

Baur, Susan. *The Intimate Hour: Love and Sex in Psychotherapy.* NY: Houghton Mifflin, 1997.

Bayer, R. *Homosexuality and American Psychiatry: The Politics of Diagnosis.* NY: Basic Books, 1981.

Bodecker, A. *My View.* The National Psychologist, 1994.

Bollas, Christopher. *The New Informants: The Betrayal of Confidentiality in Psychoanalysis and Psychotherapy.* NJ: Jason Aronson, 1996.

Breggin, Peter R. and Ginger Ross Breggin. *Talking Back to Prozac: What Doctors Aren't Telling You About Today's Most Controversial Drug.* NY: St. Martin's Press, 1994.

Breggin, Peter R. *Toxic Psychiatry: Why Therapy, Empathy, and Law Must Replace Drugs, Electroshock, and Biochemical Theories of the "New" Psychiatry.* NY: St. Martin's Press, 1991.

Breggin, Peter R. *The War against Children: How the Drug Programs and Theories of the Psychiatric Establishment Are Threatening America's Children with a Medical Cure for Violence.* NY: St. Martin's Press, 1994.

Browne, Susan E., Debra Connors, and Nancy Stern, eds. *With the Power of Each Breath: A Disabled Women's Anthology.* CA: Cleis Press, 1985.

Burstow, Bonnie and Don Weitz, eds. *Shrink Resistant: The Struggle Against Psychiatry in Canada.* Vancouver: New Star

Publications, 1988.

Campbell, T. W. *Beware of the Talking Cure. Psychotherapy May Be Hazardous to Your Mental Health.* FL: Upton Books, 1994.

Caplan, Paula J. *They Say You're Crazy: How the World's Most Powerful Psychiatrists Decide Who's Normal.* MA: Addison Wesley, 1995.

Chafetz, Gary S. and Morris E. Chafetz. *Obsession: The Bizarre Relationship Between a Prominent Harvard Psychiatrist and Her Suicidal Patient.* NY: Crown, 1994.

Chesler, Phyllis. *Women and Madness.* NY: Harcourt Brace Jovanovich, 1989.

Cohen, David, ed. *Challenging the Therapeutic State: Critical Perspectives on Psychiatry and the Mental Health System.* NY: Institute of Mind and Behavior Press, 1990. For ordering information, write to *journal,* P.O. Box 522, Village Station, New York, NY 10014.

Cohen, David, ed. *Challenging the Therapeutic State, Part 2: Further Disquisitions on the Mental Health System.* Montreal: University of Montreal, 1994.

Coleman, Lee. *The Reign of Error: Psychiatry, Authority and Law.* MA: Beacon Press, 1984.

Crews, Frederick and His Critics. *The Memory Wars: Freud's Legacy in Dispute.* NY: New York Review of Books, 1995.

Dawes, Robyn M. *House of Cards: Psychology and Psychotherapy Built on Myth.* NY: Free Press, 1994.

Donaldson, Kenneth. *Insanity Inside Out.* NY: Crown, 1976. Donaldson, who was committed against his will to the Florida State Hospital at Chattahoochee, where he remained for fifteen years, is the first American psychiatric patient ever to win damages against his physicians, as well as the first to have his case heard by the United States Supreme Court. His book brings to the fore the issue of patients' civil rights.

Dossey, Larry. *Healing Words the Power of Prayer and Practice of Medicine.* NY: Harper Collins, 1995.

Ekstein, Rudolf. *Teaching and Learning Psychotherapy.* Universities Press, 1972.

Farber, Seth. *Madness, Heresy and the Rumor of Angels: The Revolt Against the Mental Health System.* IL: Open Court, 1993.

Ferenczi, S. *Psycho-Analysis and Criminology.* London: Hogarth, 1950.

Figert, Anne E. *Women and the Ownership of PMS: The Structuring of a Psychiatric Disorder.* NY: Aldine De Gruyter, 1996.

Freeman, Lucy. *The True Story of the First Woman to Successfully Sue Her Psychiatrist for Using Sex in the Guise of Therapy.* Book World Promotions, 1976.

Gabbard, Glen. *Sexual Exploitations in Professional Relationships.* Washington D.C.: American Psychiatric Press, 1989.

Geller, Jeffrey L. and Maxine Harris. *Women of the Asylum: Voices from behind the Walls, 1840-1945.* NY: Anchor Books, 1994.

Gotkin, Janet and Paul Gotkin. *Too Much Anger, Too Many Tears: A Personal Triumph over Psychiatry.* NY: Quadrangle, 1975.

Grobe, Jeannie, ed.. *Beyond Bedlam: Contemporary Women Psychiatric Survivors Speak Out.* Third Side Press, 1995.

Gross, Martin L. *Psychological Society: A Critical Analysis of Psychiatry, Psychotherapy, Psychoanalysis and the Psychological Revolution.* NY: Random House, 1978.

Horney, Karen. *Self–Analysis.* NY: Norton, 1994.

Jehu, Derek, et.el. *Patients As Victims: Sexual Abuse in Psychotherapy and Counseling.* NY: John Wiley & Sons, 1994.

Johnston, Paul. *Quest for God: A Personal Pilgrimage.* NY: Harpercollins, 1996.

Johnstone, Lucy. *Users and Abusers of Psychiatry: A Critical Look at Traditional Psychiatric Practice.* London and New York: Routledge, 1989.

Kirk, Stuart A. and Herb Kutchins. *The Rhetoric of Science in Psychiatry (Social Problems and Social Issues).* NY: Aldine De Gruyter, 1992.

Kelly, James L. *Psychiatric Malpractice: Stories of Patients, Psychiatrists, and the Law.* NJ: Rutgers University Press, 1996.

Kovel, J. *A. Critique of the DSM–III.* Research in Law, Deviance, and Social Control, 1988.

Loftus, Elizabeth and Katherine Ketcham. *The Myth of Repressed*

Memory: False Memory and Allegations of Sexual Abuse. NY: St. Martin's Press, 1994.

Masson, Jeffrey M. *Against Therapy*. ME: Common Courage Press, 1994.

Masson, Jeffrey M. *The Assault on Truth: Freud's Suppression of the: Seduction Theory*. NY: Viking–Penguin, 1985.

McCullough, Christopher J. and Kristin Anundsen. *Nobody's Victim: Freedom from Therapy and Recovery*. NY: Clarkson Potter, 1995.

McManus, Michael. *Ethics and Religion*. FL: Herald, 1996.

McNarmara, Eileen. *Breakdown: Sex Suicide, and the Harvard Psychiatrist*. NY: Pocket Books, 1994.

Medawar, P. *Victims of Psychiatry*. New York Review of Books, 1975.

Menninger, K. *The Vital Balance: The Life Process in Mental Health and Illness*. NY: Viking, 1963.

Mithers, Carol L. *Therapy Gone Mad: The True Story of Hundreds of Patients and a Generation of Betrayal*. MA: Addison–Wesley, 1994.

Ossoff, Jon. *In the Cavern of the Demon of the Black Mountain: A Meditation of Oppression, Betrayal and the Tyranny of Control*. Laurel Canyon Press, 1995.

Ofshe, Richard and Ethan. *Making Monsters: False Memories, Psychotherapy, and Sexual Hysteria*. NY: Scribner, 1994.

Peck, Scott M. *A World Waiting to be Born*. NY: Bantam, 1994.

Plaisl, Ellen. *Therapist: The Shocking Autobiography of a Woman Sexually Exploited by Her Analyst*. NY: St. Martin's/Marek, 1985.

Pendergrast, Mark. *Victims of Memory: Incest Accusations and Shattered Lives*. Hinesburg. VT: Upper Access Books, 1995.

Phillips, Adam. *Terror and Expert*. MA: Harvard University Press, 1996.

Pope, Kenneth and Jacqueline Bouhoutsos. *Sexual Intimacy between Therapists and Patients*. NY: Praeger, 1986.

Russell, Janice. *Out of Bounds: Sexual Exploitation in Counseling and Therapy*. Sage, 1993.

Rutter, Peter. *Sex in the Forbidden Zone: When Men in Power-Therapists, Doctors, Clergy, Teachers and Others-Betray*

Women's Trust. CA: Tarcher, 1989.

Shepard, Martin. *The Love Treatment: Sexual Intimacy Between Patients and Psychotherapists*. NY: Wyden, 1971.

Siegel, Bernie. *Love, Medicine and Miracles*. NY: Harper Collins, 1990.

Singer, Margaret T. and Janja Lalich. *'Crazy' Therapies: What Are They? Do They Work?* CA: Jossey–Bass, 1996.

Smith, Susan. *Survivor Psychology: The Dark Side of a Mental Health Mission.* Social Issue Resource Series, 1995.

Strean, Herbert S. *Therapists Who Have Sex With Their Patients: Treatment and Recovery.* NY: Brunner/Mazel, 1993.

Sutherland, Pamela K. *Sexual Abuse by Therapists, Physicians, Attorneys, and Other Professionals.* WWLIA, 1996.

Sugar, Frank E. *Mindrape.* NY: Exposition, 1978.

Szasz, Thomas S. *Cruel Compassion: Psychiatric Control of Societies Unwanted.* NY: John Wiley & Sons, 1994.

Szasz, Thomas S. *Ideology and Insanity: Essays on the Psychiatric Dehumanization of Man.* NY: Syracuse University Press, 1991.

Szasz, Thomas S. *The Myth of Mental Illness: Foundations of a Theory of Personal Conduct.* NY: Hoeber–Harper, 1961.

Szasz, Thomas S. The Myth of Psychotherapy: Mental Healing As Religion, Rhetoric, and Repression. NY: Anchor Press, 1978.

Tallis, R.C. *Burying Freud.* The Lancet, 1996.

Tennow, Dorthy. *Psychotherapy: The Hazardous Cure*. NY: Anchor Books, 1976.

Ussher, Jane. *Women's Madness: Misogyny or Mental Illness.* MA: University of Massachusetts Press, 1992.

Vonnegut, Mark. *The Eden Express.* NY: Praeger, 1975.

Wood, Garth. *The Myth of Neurosis: Overcoming the Illness Excuse.* NY: Harper & Row, 1989.

Wood, Mary Elene. *The Writing on the Wall: Women Autobiography and the Asylum.* IL: University of Illinois Press, 1994.

Webster, R. *Why Freud was Wrong, Sin, Science and Psycho-analysis.* London: Harper Collins, 1995.

ORDERING

Therapeutic Madness

Visa, Master Card, American Express Card Holders Toll Free

1-888-265-2732

Non-Credit Card Check or Money Orders

Verlager Books
P.O. Box 143
Lyme Center, NH 03769

Therapeutic Madness		$12.95
Postage		$ 1.50
Total		$14.45

Name_____Address_____

City_____State_____Zip_____

Bookstores and Distributors call
1-888-265-2732
OR
1-888-626-6575

Multi-book discounts
E-Mail: verlager.books @valley.net

Verlager Audio

THERAPEUTIC MADNESS

By Mail

Pop the audio cassette into your car stereo or listen to it at home. Hours of intrigue, entertainment, and self-help information.

Therapeutic Madness	$16.00
Postage and Handling	$ 1.50
Total	$17.50

Allow 2 weeks delivery

Name_____Address_____
City_____State_____ Zip_____

Send check or   Verlager Books
Money order to: P.O. Box 143
                    Lyme Center, NH 03769

credit card orders toll free   1-888-626-6575